T3-BOX-426

To
my loving wife, Beth

To
Sarah, Brian, and Mark
who are not at all impressed that their daddy wrote this book

A special thank you
to the members of Immanuel Christian Reformed Church, Ripon, California,
for test piloting this material,
and for their helpful suggestions and support.

WHEN HURTS GO DEEP

HELPING

EACH

OTHER

IN TIMES

OF CRISIS

by Thomas L. Haan

CRC Publications
Grand Rapids, Michigan

Acknowledgments

Cover illustration: Paul Stoub

Unless otherwise indicated, the Scripture quotations in this publication are from the Holy Bible, New International Version. Copyright © 1973, 1978, 1984, International Bible Society. Used by permission of Zondervan Bible Publishers.

Copyright © 1995 by CRC Publications, 2850 Kalamazoo Ave. SE, Grand Rapids, Michigan 49560.

All rights reserved. With the exception of brief excerpts for review purposes, no part of this book may be reproduced in any manner whatsoever without written permission from the publisher. Printed in the United States of America on recycled paper. ♻

Library of Congress Cataloging-in-Publication Data
Haan, Thomas L., 1958-
    When hurts go deep: helping each other in times of crisis/
Thomas L. Haan.
      p.   cm.
    Includes bibliographical references (p.).
    ISBN 1-56212-106-5
    1. Life change events—Religious aspects—Christianity.
2. Christian life.   I. Title.
BV4509.5.H22 1995
248.8'6—dc20   95-16263
                                              CIP

10 9 8 7 6 5 4 3 2 1

TABLE OF CONTENTS

INTRODUCTION

In recent years practical books on marriage and family, dealing with issues such as problem solving, conflict resolution, communication, and changing roles have become popular. Although these are interesting and appropriate topics, when crises come into our lives, we need a far deeper understanding of what we are experiencing and how we are to deal with them.

While writing this course, I had three goals in mind:

- To inform you about crises in general and some crises you may encounter;
- To encourage you to seek help when experiencing crises;
- To equip you to help others in crisis.

In his ministry Jesus brought his healing presence into the pain-filled lives of many people. We can learn much from the way Jesus worked. Sympathetically discerning people's true needs, he was compassionate and accepting. At the same time he confronted people and made them accept responsibility for turning from their present condition. In all that he did and said, Jesus helped people to have peace of mind and hope that their lives could be fulfilling if they believed in him.

Jesus' ministry was so effective because he not only came to do the Father's will but also lived the life of faith he preached. He was not afraid to get involved in the lives of rejected people. And his personal life was characterized by prayer and dependence on the strength of the Holy Spirit.

Before ascending into heaven, Jesus told his disciples that he would send another comforter, the Holy Spirit, to lead and guide them into all truth. His last words to them were, "And surely I will be with you always to the very end of the age."

The Lord is always with us, in the happy and in the stressful times, and even when our worlds are falling apart. He speaks to us through the Word, through prayer, and by means of the Holy Spirit. We can also feel his presence in our lives through those who come to minister to us in his name. Jesus' disciples on this earth continue his ministry as they serve those in crisis.

Chapter One

WHAT IS A CRISIS?

CHANDLER, MINNESOTA: Residents of this tiny southwestern Minnesota town are cleaning up debris and rebuilding homes that were destroyed on June 16. At 5:17 p.m. a tornado churned through town, demolishing businesses and houses. Pastor John Engbers estimated that about one-third of his congregation of eighty families lost their homes.

EDMONTON, ALBERTA, CANADA: A twenty-five-foot fall from the roof of Bethel Church left a volunteer worker paralyzed and close to death. Project manager Jim Rietveld knew the moment he reached Jack Tabak, the fallen worker, that he was in serious condition. "I felt that Jack was close to death when I got to him," said Rietveld.

KANSAS CITY, MISSOURI: Brenda Wassink, 22, had a good life and a glowing future. On May 11, Brenda was walking through a Wal-Mart parking lot in suburban Kansas City when a woman approached her and tried to grab her purse. When Brenda resisted, the women shot her in the head. Brenda died about three hours later during surgery at a local hospital. The murder sent shock waves through the small congregation in Kansas City.

These three events, reported in the church periodical, *The Banner*, all describe crisis situations. While different in many ways, they contain common elements that can help us understand what forms a crisis in our lives.

Crises begin with a **hazardous event**. Something unexpected happens: a tornado rips through a town, a man falls off a roof, a girl is murdered. People's lives are changed dramatically and will never be the same.

Crises happen to people in a **vulnerable state**. Not everyone in Chandler experienced an emotional trauma of crisis proportions. Some were warned early enough to find safety, and others had experienced tornadoes before and knew what to expect. A person must be vulnerable for a crisis to occur. Being tired from overwork or depressed because of a recent childbirth can prevent a person from handling a situation that she ordinarily could deal with without difficulty. Or the hazardous event may be so tragic, like Brenda Wassink's murder, that it immediately drains those involved of all possible strength.

Crises are also characterized by a **precipitating factor**. Something becomes the straw that broke the camel's back. That may be an event that predictably would break anyone—the shock of witnessing a family member's pain. Or it could be an unexpected event that seems so small; there are people, for example, who are strong during a time of extreme loss and then fall apart over a missing button.

A combination of these elements—hazardous event, vulnerable state, and precipitating factor—can result in a state of active crisis, in which a person cannot deal with the situation any longer. An active crisis is characterized by the following:

- Stress, psychological and/or physical
  The consequence may be depression, headaches, or ulcers.

- Panic and defeat
  At this stage a person feels that nothing in his life works; he is a failure, without hope. Some people become agitated—pacing, drinking alcohol, taking drugs, driving fast, or getting in fights; others become apathetic, sleeping the day away.

- A need for relief
  Since it is impossible for people in this state to deal with the problem in a rational way, they may appear dazed or exhibit bizarre behavior. They look to others for help.

- Inefficiency
  People in crisis often cannot function normally but act at about sixty percent of their physical and emotional ability. Dealing with the loss of a loved one may result in constant tears or in work that proceeds at a snail's pace.

A Biblical View

We who live in the information age seem to have more difficulty handling crises than our ancestors did. Modern science has fostered the illusion that we can live relatively crisis-free lives; when that illusion is shattered, emotional trauma can be enormous.

Crises force us to make choices, which are fundamentally religious or faith decisions. Those who have turned away from God are left to struggle with whatever human defense is possible, whether that be denial or superhuman courage.

Not that Christians are free of crises or breeze right through them because of their faith. Brenda Wassink's fiancé, Joel, for example, is struggling to understand a future that has suddenly turned upside down. For answers he turns to passages in Scripture that now are taking on new meaning. Jeremiah 29:11, which he and Brenda chose for their wedding passage, is one of them: " 'For I know the plans I have for you,' declares the Lord, 'plans to prosper you and not to harm you, plans to give you hope and a future.' "

"I'm still not sure what to do with that," Joel says.

The Bible presents us with an understanding of crisis that empowers us to be "more than conquerors through [the Lord] who loved us" (Rom. 8:37). The Bible's answer to crises is neither denial nor superhuman courage. It is faith in what we are taught about God and his relationship to his covenant people.

As Christians we believe that God created, rules, and upholds the world. Accordingly, every crisis is under God's control. This perception raises many questions, some of which we will never be able to answer, but it also provides the comfort that nothing happens to us that is outside of God's control.

Where then do crisis events come from?

Crises may be the result of God's specific intervention in a person's life. The apostle Paul's conversion provides a good example. On the way to Damascus to persecute Christians, Paul was confronted with a bright light and the voice of Jesus from heaven. All the elements described earlier of a crisis event were present. Paul became a blind, defeated man, not eating or drinking for three days.

Therefore, crises are not always bad nor do they always lead to negative outcomes. The Chinese character that represents the idea of *crisis* combines two symbols, one for despair and another for opportunity. Even though the crisis itself may cause pain, the outcome can be good, as it was in Paul's life.

All Christians need to be constantly open to God's call to change. Peter, James, and John undoubtedly thought they were doing God's work by fishing, but Jesus shook up their comfortable existences and called them to be fishers of men. The Bible is filled with other stories of God's direct intervention in people's lives, which caused crises: consider the stories of Moses, Pharaoh, and Nebuchadnezzer.

Crises may enter our lives through the natural progression of creation and time. God created the earth to function in a way that includes earthquakes, floods, tornadoes, hurricanes, and fires. Scripture provides no evidence that natural disasters are the direct result of the fall. All of these events can occasion a crisis, but we should not assume they occur because God and creation are against us.

The Bible tells us in Genesis 1 that humans are the crown of creation, made in God's image. Through his covenants God enters into a special relationship with us, which binds us together. Creation is called to serve that covenant relationship.

The Bible does show God using creation, as in the case of the flood, to punish humans who live outside his divine will. In Deuteronomy 28 the Lord tells the people of Israel that covenant faithfulness will mean abundant crops, but unfaithfulness will bring famine and drought.

In Luke 13 and John 9, however, Jesus corrected the erroneous idea that natural disaster and illness are always the direct result of someone's sin. Can we possibly conclude that God sent a tornado to Chandler, Minnesota, to punish those residents for their sin?

In Revelation the apostle John describes his visions of earthquakes and fires; these visions tell us that natural disasters are used by God as warnings to all people to make sure they are right with the Lord.

As we reflect upon a crisis caused by a natural disaster, we can also often see God's graciousness to us. "It's truly amazing that no one was killed in the storm. We see the Lord's hand so clearly here," the pastor of the Chandler church said. "If the storm had come during the night, there's no telling what might have happened."

Many crises also come as a result of the natural cycle of life—birth, childhood, adolescence, adulthood, middle age, retirement, and death. Everyone experiences life adjustments at each of these stages, and for some the transition from one stage to the next can be traumatic. Such crises are not evil by nature but simply the way life is after the fall.

Some crises come as a result of sin, either our own or someone else's. His personal sin resulted in a crisis both in King David's own family and in the lives of others. Stephen faced the crisis of death, not because of his own sin but because of others' sinful rejection of his testimony. We all know people—perhaps you are one—who have been the victims of sin that brought crime, divorce, rape, or financial loss into their lives.

But God is a God of purpose. We can be sure that everything that takes place in our world is part of his plan to bring the kingdom of God to its intended fulfillment.

Although God created the world without sin, he permitted sin to enter, and he works with the results of sin, as we must also. God even uses evil to bring about his purposes in the world. The Belgic Confession, Article 13, states:

> We believe that this good God,
>   after he created all things,
> did not abandon them to chance or fortune
> but leads and governs them
>   according to his holy will,
> in such a way that nothing happens in this world
> without his orderly arrangement.

Yet God is not the author of,
nor can be charged with,
the sin that occurs.
For his power and goodness
are so great and incomprehensible
that he arranges and does his work very well and justly
even when the devils and evil men act unjustly.

In this thought we rest,
knowing that he holds in check
the devils and all our enemies,
    who cannot hurt us
    without his permission and will.

As citizens of God's kingdom we can be sure that the events of our lives are part of God's plan to fulfill that kingdom. We are under the loving care of a God who has bonded himself to us for our good.

We cannot, of course, always choose our circumstances, but we can choose our attitude toward those circumstances. When we experience difficulties, we can look at them in either a helpful or a destructive way. We can become angry with God for allowing such a cruel thing to occur. We can become bitter and resentful. We can turn our anger inward, blame ourselves, and spend the rest of our years punishing ourselves. We can decide life has no meaning and wander in unbelief. Or we can move ahead in faith using God-given and life-giving resources.

One such resource is the knowledge that God is good. Crises create uncertainty. But when a person knows God is love and his love will never change, that idea gives a sense of security in a world of constant change. Remembering that God is good can help us through the "it isn't fair" situations, such as the death of a child or spouse. Through our pain we can know that our dear ones are in the arms of our loving Father and that those strong arms hold us as well.

Another resource during times of crisis is prayer. Our prayer ought not to be, "Lord, get me out of this mess"; the Bible tells us to pray for the Lord's will to be done. Our prayer should rather be, "Help us to know you and be sensitive to your leading through this crisis." Prayer brings God into our problem-filled lives and allows us to grow spiritually. At times God works miraculously—and we should pray for miracles—but at other times the power of God is manifested through the faith of his saints as they endured crises (2 Cor.12:7-10).

For Christians the Holy Spirit is a rock to which they can cling in times of trouble. Jesus said that he would never leave us or forsake us, and the Holy Spirit is the presence of Christ living within us. We need the Spirit's power when all our own power seems to have been taken away.

Still another important source of strength is the church, the body of Christ. Many people in the world suffer through illness and grief alone, but Christians need not do so. When going through crises, out of embarrassment or pride, we often tend to pull away from our friends, but that should be precisely the time we cling to them for help and guidance.

All of these resources are presented to us in the Bible, our source of guidance and comfort during times of crisis. Often the Word of God is more real to us during crises than in a catechism class or when we are listening to a sermon. Then the Bible touches our lives, not just our minds, and shows us the love and care of a God who is with us in the worst of times.

What's Happening To Me?

The following chart, developed by Norman Wright, can help us to understand the different phases of a crisis.

CHANGE AND CRISIS SEQUENCE				
Phases	*Phase I*	*Phase II*	*Phase III*	*Phase VI*
	Impact	Withdrawal, Confusion	Adjustment	Reconstruction, Reconciliation

Emotional Level — EMOTIONAL LEVEL (curve showing emotional level declining through Phase II and recovering through Phase VI)

Time	*Hours*	*Days*	*Weeks*	*Months*
Response	Fight, Flight	Anger, Fear, Guilt, Rage	Positive thoughts begin	Hope
Thought	Numbness, Disorientation	Ambiguity, Uncertainty	Problem solving	Consolidation of problem solving
Direction	Search for lost object	Bargaining, Detachment	Search for new object	Reattachment
Search Behavior	Reminiscence	Perplexed scanning	Focused exploration	Reality testing
Guidance Needed	Acceptance of feeling	Task-oriented direction	Support, Spiritual insight	Breakthrough, Reinforce hope

Impact Phase

In this phase a person feels like she has been clouted with a two-by-four. It is usually a painful but brief time, which may last only a few hours or a few days, a time when a person becomes aware of the tragedy that has entered her life.

She faces a choice, whether to stay and fight the problem through to resolution or to run and ignore it. Psychologists call this the "fight-or-flight pattern." If a person's tendency has been to face problems, she will probably face this one as well. But if her tendency has been to avoid them, she will probably run. Staying and attempting to deal with the problem is the healthier response.

During this phase, capacity for thought is greatly diminished. The person is numb and disoriented. Her entire body may seem shut down. That's normal and good—a kind of psychic shock absorber. At this point it would be too damaging to the system to accept the full impact.

Factual information given people in the impact stage won't be fully comprehended; it must often be repeated later. Important decisions may be unavoidable, but they may be made unwisely. The help of other caring people is essential at this time.

When a person first faces a tragic situation, she is actually and symbolically searching for the lost object. She may, for example, take out old photographs and reminisce about the person who has died. It is important for everyone involved to express feelings—anger, sadness, guilt. And this is a time for nonjudgmental listening by friends and family.

When feelings are denied or rejected in the early days of a crisis, the resolution will often be delayed. Cultural and religious background may effect a person's ability to properly express grief—such expression may be seen as a lack of faith. But such a belief can lead to bottled up feelings and years of guilt, anger, and sadness.

How often haven't you heard this conversation at a funeral?

"How is Mary doing?"

"Oh, we are so proud of her, she is taking it so well."

"Yes, we need to have faith that all things work for the good of those who love the Lord, don't we?"

This conversation assumes that Mary has deep faith because she hasn't expressed any negative emotions. Such thinking is unbiblical and unhealthy. Mary is actually pushing her feelings deep down inside because she does not want people to think she is weak. Jesus' weeping at the tomb of Lazarus demonstrates there is no direct link between faith and public grieving.

We're often uncomfortable when someone is crying or expressing unhappiness. But if we succumb to that feeling, we are imposing our own feelings, perhaps our own fear of dying, on the grieving person. By accepting our fears and allowing the other person to express their feelings during this initial stage, we will help to bring the crisis to a resolution.

Withdrawal-Confusion Phase

A diminished emotional level is common at this time. The person may be extremely fatigued or suffer depression for days or even weeks. (Note: Each new phase on the chart is progressively longer.) Suppressing anger, fear, and guilt, he may not know what to feel or may not want to deal with his feelings. The support of other Christians is so important. They must be good listeners, but they should also perform physical tasks that the person is unable to do.

This is also a time of confusion for the person in crisis. He may, for example, begin a task and, for no apparent reason, fail to complete it. He may also approach others and then back away. There is still a yearning to replace what is lost in his life. For obvious reasons, major, life-changing decisions should not be made now.

Adjustment Phase

The adjustment phase usually lasts for weeks or even months. At this point the person begins to feel hope. Depression will come and go, but things are beginning to look up. She may talk about starting a new job, moving to a new location, rebuilding a fire-destroyed home, or meeting new people. She is completing her detachment from the lost object or person and looking for new things or people to become attached to.

Ups and downs will still occur, however, and the person in crisis will need someone close by she can trust. This is also a time when she is most open to new spiritual insights and to a deepening of her beliefs.

Reconstruction-Reconciliation Phase

At this point the person has a new sense of self-assurance and can plan confidently. Feelings of doubt and self-pity are gone because she has made a conscious choice not to engage in such feelings anymore. New attachments are secured—new people, new places, new activities, new jobs, and new spiritual responses and depths. Anger and blame are set aside, and broken relationships are healed. She may begin to write letters, invite people over for meals, or do helpful tasks as a form of reconciliation.

Children's Responses

A stressful situation that does not trigger a crisis for an adult may do so for a child. Moving, parental divorce, rejection by a friend, loss of a pet, or a poor grade on a test can produce emotions so intense that a crisis occurs. Long-lasting effects are possible because the crisis may make the child less capable of dealing with stressful situations in the future.

Children deal with crises differently than adults do. Typically, they experience two stages of crisis resolution. First, they feel an initial shock and a high level of anxiety. They lack coping skills to solve the problem they face. Adults can fall back on routines and developed resources; children fall back on chaos, often losing their sense of identity.

The second stage is similar to but less intense than the first. At this point children are able to evaluate the crisis instead of just respond to it. But they lack verbal skills, and they still cannot see available options. Thus they feel totally helpless in the strange and fearful situation. Children need to talk to and sort out their fears with a compassionate, understanding adult.

A characteristic response of a child in crisis is regression. A ten-year-old, whose parent is suffering from a serious illness, may become clingy, have fits, wet the bed, and fear being alone in the dark. Not understanding that regression is a natural way for a child to deal with crisis, adults often see the child's behavior as an unwanted additional stress for themselves.

Parents must understand that a child can sense when something is wrong with a loved one. The notion that "if you don't tell them the problem, they won't worry about it" is false. It's best is to be open and honest. Children should be given repeated assurances of love and be told in simple terms as much as they need to know.

Children's responses will also vary according to their age. Three-to-six-year-old children are egocentric—a natural stage in their development. They think that they can influence events through their thoughts. If they become ill, they may believe that they have caused the illness or that they are being punished for doing something bad. If a parent becomes ill, they may think that they caused that to occur as well.

Young children also make unique connections that make sense to them but to no one else. For example, if his mother comes home in pain after playing softball, a boy may relate the pain with the game. The next time his father asks him to play softball in the backyard, he may not want to play. It is important to help children understand that they do not cause crisis events to happen and need not be anxious.

Children from ages seven to twelve have developed the ability to think conceptually; they can work out problems in their minds instead of relying on trial and error. They no longer believe that their thoughts can cause things to happen. They can now accept the viewpoints and recognize the feelings of others. However, they often try to hide their own feelings. It's important to be sensitive and nonjudgmental, compassionately drawing out their fears and questions. Openness and honesty are keys to helping children through times of crisis.

Staying on Top of a Crisis

Unable to cope with life and its stresses, some people seem to be crisis-prone. But even for those who appear to sail through life on continuously calm seas, certain factors can make them vulnerable to a crisis in their lives. To avoid such crises, people need to have the following:

An Adequate Perception of the Situation

The ability to keep an objective perspective on a situation is one factor that determines how well a person copes. For example, a parent who discovers that her son or daughter has a drug problem may feel this to be the greatest possible tragedy and a negative commentary on her child-raising ability. But another parent in a similar situation may perceive that the child's upbringing is one factor among many that could be contributing to the predicament.

Past experiences also have a bearing on our perceptions. If a stressful situation is related to an unresolved crisis, then the new stress only serves to bring back old hurts. Job loss is always stressful, but if poor self-esteem is part of the equation, such a time could turn into a crisis.

To maintain an adequate perception of the situation it is important to recognize that most crises involve a tremendous sense of loss and that it is essential to identify the loss.

A person's self-esteem is often dealt a serious blow at this time. If he has lost his job, if his child is in jail, if his marriage is broken, he may feel like a complete failure and will worry that others will not continue to accept him.

Life changes often necessitate a reevaluation of who one is, and for some this is very difficult. Thus crisis events can also result in a loss of identity. For example, if a woman's life and energy has been focused on her children for thirty years, and the children are now grown and have moved on, she may ask herself: "Now what will I do with my time? Who am I now if I am not a mother?" Because men in contemporary American culture often find their sense of identity in their work, retirement can cause a painful identity loss for them.

Another loss that may be a precipitating factor in a crisis concerns role mastery. If a person has mastered a specific function at work, home, or church, and then is asked to turn to a new task, this loss can cause a crisis.

Because we cannot live without some form of nurturance, a major cause of crises is its loss. As basic as the need for food and shelter is the need to be part of a group, to have people who care about us. Consequently, one of the most stressful events in life is the loss of a spouse. But moving away from family and friends as well as changing jobs can also cause stress.

An Adequate Social Network

Another important factor in one's ability to cope in times of crisis is an adequate social network. Does the person have relatives and friends who can help her through this time? Loneliness just compounds the problem. The cruelty and pain of the cross were greatly enhanced by Jesus' sense that his Father had forsaken him. He was all alone. His support network was shattered. During times of crisis the body of Christ can be the greatest support group available if it can respond to a person in need.

Research has shown that the average family goes through a moderate to severe crisis every three to four years. This means that half of the families in a congregation are either in active crisis or are dealing with a past crisis. How can the pastoral staff or the elders be expected to handle all these situations in a congregation? The body of Christ, as a whole, must be mobilized to minister to those in crisis and not leave this ministry to a few.

The people involved in the tragic events described at the beginning of this chapter testified to the wonderful support they received from their churches:

"I've had excellent medical care, and my church and my friends are praying for me."

"We are so appreciative of all the help we've received." "There are a lot of bighearted people out there."

"We have been overwhelmed by the letters and phone calls we've received from people we don't know. We have been lifted up."

But the Christian community has not always been the support network it was intended to be, and often the reason is not because people are unwilling to help. Some Christians believe that they must put on a good front. If crisis events do arise, they will not seek the vital help of the Christian community because that would reveal that their lives are not as good and prosperous as they would have others believe.

At times Christians assume that whatever difficult situation comes into their lives is the cross God asks them to bear. They feel they must be strong, never asking for support or help because that would show lack of faith. These two responses are typical of those of us who are descendants of the Dutch.

That heritage has often resulted in isolation from those around us, and that type of thinking is displayed on the congregational, family, and individual level. Emotionally stalwart, we tend to be a private people; problems were historically dealt with between father and son in the barn while milking the cows or between mother and daughter in the house doing the dishes—if they were dealt with at all. Even though we have become a largely urban people, that mentality still prevails.

Fortunately, there are notable exceptions. When physical illness or death occurs, if somebody's house catches on fire or some other physical disaster happens, we often provide great support. But the same unconditional love is often not present if a person suffers from an emotional problem or a family has a serious dysfunction.

Throughout our history we have not only been suspect of emotionalism but of emotion itself. Our spirituality has been kept on an intellectual plane. Emotional or family problems have been viewed as too frightening to express to the body of Christ. And people with these kinds of difficulties are, at times, viewed as contagious or dangerous. Our refrain has often been, "Don't put out your dirty laundry for all the world to see."

If the body of Christ is going to provide support, we must accept one another as imperfect and broken in our personal and family lives as well as in our spiritual lives. That means communicating feelings with one another as well as recognizing that we are emotional as well as intellectual beings. And that means understanding that a dysfunctional family has as great and legitimate a crisis as a family that suffers from ill health or death.

We also have to resist the temptation to isolate ourselves in times of crisis; we must be willing to ask for prayer and to receive the support of fellow Christians. The greater the crisis the larger the network that is needed. A desire to separate ourselves from others at these times only demonstrates the depth of our emotional poverty.

The growing diversity in my own denomination also affects our ability to provide adequate support networks. The Dutch who came to the United States and formed our church greatly resisted Americanization. Their language and culture were the glue that held them together. Even after the last Dutch worship services ended in the 1960s, the group's Dutchness was still very noticeable. Although it is important to appreciate one's roots, many in this tradition still look upon those who are not Dutch as outsiders and hesitate to include them in their social support network.

Studies indicate that within the next twenty years many ethnic groups will become part of our denominational fellowship, and the Dutch may not necessarily be the predominate group. If our churches are going to provide the support so important in the body of Christ, we must appreciate this diversity, praise God for it, and accept one another as brothers and sisters in Christ no matter what our ethnic heritage.

Adequate Coping Mechanisms

How well a person overcomes difficulties in times of crisis also depends upon his coping mechanisms. Such mechanisms could include the ability to reason out the problem, to find helpful information, and to find strength in Bible reading or prayer.

Two important practical coping skills involve problem solving and communication. Many people could avoid crises if they knew how to examine a problem and come up with various alternatives to find the solution. A crisis can also be fueled when a person cannot adequately express what he feels or needs. Poor communication skills can turn a fearful and frustrating situation into a shouting match—or worse.

Thus if a person has an adequate perception of the stressful situation, an adequate social network, and adequate coping mechanisms, a crisis can be avoided or greatly minimized. But if one or more of these balancing factors are absent or are insufficient, then a crisis is probably inevitable.

FOR PERSONAL PREPARATION

To help absorb some of the information in this first chapter and to prepare for the group session, try to recall a crisis that occurred in your life or in the life of someone close to you. Did it match or differ from the descriptions above? Did you experience the four phases in the chart? Were you able to stay on top of the crisis? What helped you cope?

Next consider how your understanding of God and your relationship to God affected your understanding of and your coping with that crisis.

Chapter Two

THE CRISIS OF ILLNESS

After the Wednesday night youth group meeting the adult leaders usually stayed to discuss the events of the evening and to prepare for the next meeting. One night the discussion was interrupted by an urgent phone call for Steve or Kathy. After answering the call, Kathy reappeared with fear in her eyes. "Lucas had a seizure," she said. "The ambulance is on its way!" Quickly Steve and Kathy bolted for the door and raced home.

For most adults the headaches, stomachaches, colds, and flu of family members does not precipitate a crisis. It may cause stress and adjustment for a few hours or even days, but it does not bring the family to the brink of crisis. When a life-threatening accident or illness occurs, or a family member is hospitalized, however, a crisis often results.

Illness-related Losses

Hospitals are necessary evils. Sometime in our lives—when we are ill, have an accident, or need surgery—we will probably end up in one. Hospital staff are generally professional, caring, and understanding. But the very fact that a person is in a hospital means all is not well with his life.

He may be in physical pain. He may find it difficult to sleep because of the commotion and the unfamiliar bed. The food is not always the best, and the hours can pass at a snail's pace. Emotional factors may also make a hospital stay difficult.

Loss of personal identity, for example, is a frequent by-product. When I was in college, I had to have knee surgery. Arriving at the hospital, I was asked to wait in a small cubicle for what seemed an eternity. Finally the admissions clerk came and asked my name, but it was obvious to me that she really wanted to know my social security number—the necessary information to make me an official patient.

The day after surgery I was feeling poorly. But I asked the nurse who came to empty my drainage bag for a newspaper. As she was leaving the room, I heard her say to someone that 324 would like a newspaper. I wanted to scream, "I am not 324! I am Tom Haan! I'm a student at Dordt College. I'm getting married in July. Treat me like a person."

With loss of identity comes loss of control over financial affairs. The hospital wants to know who your insurance carrier is and what percentage they will pay. After hospitalization the bills not covered by insurance arrive.

Surgery often results in the loss of a body part. Even if it's diseased, it is still part of the whole body, and there will be a period of grieving over that loss, grief that is both necessary and normal. It is difficult for those who have experienced this loss to continue to perceive of themselves as whole persons and harder yet to believe that other people will see them as such.

I once made a hospital visit to a woman who had had a hysterectomy. She was in her mid-forties and in general good health. She had five children and was not planning to have any more. But her reproductive organs were an important part of her life. They had been used by God to give her the children she loved so much. Now that was past. She realized it would take time to adjust to this new chapter in her life.

When an illness-related crisis occurs, there is often a breakdown in communication. For example, a patient may bring up some unresolved past conflict with a visiting family member or become angry with the hospital staff. Such reactions may come from feelings of negative self-worth due to the loss of personal identity, physical capability, or financial control. Medications, psychological pressures, and body-chemistry imbalances can also intensify interpersonal conflicts.

Good communication skills are essential for everyone involved in an illness-related crisis. There must be acceptance, patience, and a desire to help the patient come to grips with his sense of loss.

We're All Mortal

Many of our fears, frustrations, and expressions of anger have an important source. When we are hospitalized, we come face-to-face with our own mortality. Fear of death is true even for Christians of strong faith. We should not be ashamed to acknowledge this fear. Jesus himself admitted it in the garden of Gethsemane.

I have often been at the bedside of a Christian who was facing serious surgery, and I have heard beautiful testimonies of the assurance of salvation through faith in Jesus Christ. But in those testimonies I also heard fear that days on earth could be coming to an end.

During these times communication of emotions and feelings is necessary and a great help when important decisions must be made. Hidden feelings and questioned motivations only compound and prolong the crisis and create separate crises of their own.

Who's to Blame?

The hospitalization of a child is one of the most serious events a family can face. If an accident is the cause, there may be some blaming, either of self or of the spouse. Such faultfinding, however, only fuels the crisis and can be a smoke screen for unresolved conflict in the marriage.

Accidents happen in spite of all a loving and caring parent may do to prevent them. No one can monitor a child's actions every second of the day. When a child is hospitalized, it is not a time for blame but a time for the entire family to support one another.

On occasion the parents of a hospitalized child will panic. This only heightens the child's fear and makes the work harder for the medical staff. Because children quickly sense their parents' fears, it is important for parents to remain calm, to show an extra measure of affection, and to support both the ill child and the siblings. And all concerned should be open and honest about the patient's condition. Fear of the unknown is great for a child in the hospital, and secrecy only increases that fear.

Disabilities

Some illnesses and accidents result in temporary or permanent disabilities. With the difficulties that have already been mentioned, these conditions bring additional concerns. People may wonder, "What does the future hold?" and "How can the needed adjustments be made?"

After being released from the hospital, most disabled people continue to need physical care, which may range from help with a few minor chores to around-the-clock care. Difficult questions arise: Who is going to nurse the person when she returns home? How are the continuing medical bills going to be paid? Is someone else in the family going to have to begin to work or take on a second job? How is the disabled person going to deal with the losses? How will the family's social system be changed, especially the marriage? Will family members have different feelings about the disabled person? What job changes will the disabled person face?

If family members need to help out financially, resentment and disappointment may build, both on the part of those who help and of those being helped. Family members may feel victimized. Anger and then guilt because of the anger are frequent by-products. After all, who can get angry at a disabled person? Family members may blame themselves for the disability, and children may feel different from other children because they have a disabled parent. The impact of the disability may also result in depression and various forms of abnormal behavior by the children.

The Christian community is often not as sensitive as it should be to the needs of disabled members. A few years ago our church council considered putting a wheelchair ramp outside the building to assist those with physical challenges. I assumed there would be unanimous approval and was shocked by the response. Some council members were more concerned about the appearance of the building than they were about helping people get into the building to worship God.

The council discussion left me very curious. For many years churches have been built with basements that reach well above ground level and long flights of stairs leading up to sanctuaries. I said to an elderly member, "Congregations have always had parishioners in wheelchairs as well as those using walkers. How did these people get into church in the past?"

"Well," he replied, "I can remember the men of the church carrying old Joe up the steps, wheelchair and all. But most of those people never came to church."

Catastrophic Illness

Although facing temporary illnesses and hospitalizations can be difficult, in most cases the patient recovers and returns to his normal routine or learns to adjust to various physical disabilities. Catastrophic illness, however, is a different matter. It can cause a severe crisis in a family.

All the concerns discussed earlier are now raised to a new level. The family must deal with the very real possibility of its loved one dying or perhaps living on in a comatose state. And the family may need to decide whether or not to terminate treatment and allow the loved one to die.

October 9, 1983 is a day I will never forget. About 3 a.m. I received a phone call. A woman asked if I knew Richard Haan, who lived at 319 Vindale. I said that he was my brother. She informed me that she was calling from the hospital emergency room, and my brother had been involved in an accident. He had broken bones but was not in surgery. I told her that if they needed someone right away, my wife, Beth, was working on the fourth floor.

When I arrived at the hospital, my wife greeted me. From the look on her face I knew my brother's condition was much more serious than a "few broken bones." Beth told me that while I was on my way to the hospital an artery had ruptured in my brother's brain; he had been rushed to surgery. His life was hanging by a thread.

A physician came into the family waiting area and began to describe the seriousness of my brother's condition and the procedure the surgeons would follow. Anger welled up inside of me because the doctor was using medical jargon; I felt as if my brother's life depended on my ability to understand his words.

I then had to make the phone calls that turn a peaceful night into a nightmare. First I called my sister who lived in town. She didn't handle the news about Rich's broken bones very well, so I didn't tell her about the real danger. After I hung up, I paused for a moment hoping something would happen so I would not have to call my parents.

The phone rang in Minnesota about five times, and then I heard the familiar, "Hello, Rev. Haan speaking."

"Dad, it's me, Tom."

"Yes," he said.

"Rich has been in an accident. It doesn't look very good."

I heard the receiver clunk as it hit the wall. "Dad, Dad, are you still there?"

After a long pause he said, "Mom and I are on our way."

As I paced back and forth in the waiting room, the words of the baptism form kept running through my head, "He will avert all evil or turn it to our profit." But what good could possibly come from this? For ten days Rich lay unconscious. Only a weak squeeze of his right hand told us he was still alive.

Decisions

Because of advancements in technology many decisions in the field of medicine are now risk/benefit choices. Medicine is not a perfect science. A physician cannot look in a book and find the exact course of action to take in each situation.

In the past medical decisions were made by a physician who knew the family well and acted in its best interest. Often family members were not even involved in any decision-making process. They believed the physician would decide what was best. The foundation of this system was trust and trustworthiness.

Today the situation has changed. All authority figures have been knocked off their pedestals, including physicians. With the increase in technology has come an increase in specialization. If a person is critically ill, there will be one primary physician, who may or may not know the patient or the family. Several specialists will also be involved, who probably have never met the patient or the family. When a loved one is close to death, there is no time to get second opinions, let alone develop a trusting relationship with all the physicians involved. With less trust and more distance between physician, patient, and family, much more responsibility now rests with the patient or the family to make difficult decisions.

This change is responsible for the huge increase in malpractice suits being brought by patients against physicians. At times people sue because they are angry rather than because of actual malpractice. Some of that anger may arise because people consider it unfair that they have to make these life-and-death decisions.

Informed Consent

Before treatment can be administered or terminated by a physician, the patient or the patient's family must give informed consent. That requirement raises questions: Who determines how much information the patient or family should have, could understand, or could tolerate? Should all relevant research, treatment plans, and options be given to the patient or would that be more confusing and stressful than necessary? And what about emergency procedures? By the time all required information is given to the appropriate people, the patient could be dead. What percentage of the risk of any procedure should the patient or family be informed of?

Sometimes it is not consent but refusal to receive a treatment that becomes a problem. Is a patient competent to make such a decision? What if a legal surrogate, such as a family member, has to make the decision? How do we know she is acting in the patient's best interest?

At times the way in which physicians give their recommendations for treatment can make a difference in the decision. Older doctors tend to give orders, feeling that the patient or family cannot understand all the factors. Younger doctors tend to give options because they fear lawsuits. The problem with options, however, is that they leave the possibility of hope open and perhaps lead to more radical treatment. And the decision to terminate treatment may appear to family members to be a death wish for the patient and thus is often too difficult for them to make.

Another concern is the issue of expert knowledge. Family members assume that the physician has such knowledge (that is what they are paying for); therefore, she is better able to make an informed decision than the patient is. But what if the physician has ulterior motives? What if the procedure she is suggesting makes more profit for the hospital or the doctor? What if it is a procedure she is trained to do, and for other treatment she would have to refer the patient to another specialist?

Some years ago, experiencing abdominal pain, I was referred to a surgeon for a possible appendectomy. While attempting to procure my informed consent for the surgery, the doctor told me I had some of the signs of appendicitis but other usual symptoms were missing. When I asked him why he wanted to take out my appendix, he responded, "I'm a surgeon, that's my job." After hearing that response, I was glad I wasn't in the office of a neurosurgeon! After I refused the appendectomy, I was referred to an internist and underwent a less radical course of action. My appendix was not the problem.

Deciphering the difference between competence and capacity is another difficulty related to informed consent. In this regard the following questions should be addressed. Is the patient mentally competent to make a decision about his treatment? And is he capable of making a decision under the current circumstances? Some patients who are in great pain may make decisions that they would not make if they could think clearly.

Ultimately, a decision about treatment or the termination of treatment must be made. Who is going to make it? Who knows the mind of the patient? It is best, of course, if the patient is capable and competent and can express to the physician his own wishes, and that decision is documented in the patient's records.

If the patient is unconscious or is not capable or competent, the physician will want to know if the patient has expressed his desires in a document known as an "Advance Directive." Such a document is also called a "Durable Power of Attorney for Health Care," a "Natural Death Act Declaration," or a "Living Will." People must check with their state or province to know what document is preferred.

An "Advance Directive" is made while the patient is well and of sound mind; it expresses his wishes in the event of catastrophic illness and is to be used when the person is not capable or competent. Although an important document for a person to have, it does have its limitations. It must be updated and validated each year and cannot possibly cover every medical situation.

If the patient's wishes cannot be determined by direct communication or by an "Advance Directive," the decision falls to the family.

Imagine this scenario: family members are called into the hospital waiting room. The physician informs them of the gravity of the situation. Successful treatment appears virtually hopeless. The family is confronted with three options: (1) long-term intensive care, (2) temporary life support but with no-code orders, (3) discontinuation of life support, in which case the patient would die.

Understanding that this is not a matter of right or wrong, family members should consider several questions. What are their emotions at this time? Are they ready to let the person go? If there is some unfinished business with the patient, do they feel guilt when considering the choice of letting the person die?

In these situations family members are often angry that they have to make such a decision and in agony seeing this once dignified person reduced to an extension of machines.

Financial and social concerns may also arise. All the family finances could be wiped out. Perhaps family members feel guilty that they would allow money concerns to enter the picture. And they may worry about what other people will think of them after they make the decision.

Spiritual questions are inevitable. People may say or think: "God, this is your department, why do I have to make this decision? What if I make the wrong decision; how will I ever find forgiveness? Why do bad things happen to good people?"

This is a time when prayer and the guidance of a pastor, a mature Christian friend, or a Christian doctor or nurse can be a great help.

A Biblical Understanding

Before we are thrust into a situation of life-and-death decisions, it would be well to have a biblical understanding of human life and what it means to be human beings.

The Bible tells us we are created by God, and our life depends on his grace. "For in him we live and move and have our being," says the apostle Paul. This relationship of dependence existed even before the fall into sin.

God intended for us to have quality lives—physically, socially, and spiritually. Sin came into the world and destroyed that possibility. But we, who are Christians, know that there is hope. Jesus said, "I came that you may have life and have it abundantly." Through the death and resurrection of Jesus, Christians experience a restoration of the quality of their present lives and can look forward to a complete renewal in the new heaven and new earth.

In situations of catastrophic illness the quality of the patient's life is often the central issue. But that quality tends to be viewed in a limited way: most people see humans as merely biological/physical creatures. The very term "physician" reflects this narrow characterization. The Bible, however, shows us that we are physical, social, and spiritual beings. The complete self can only be seen as a totality of those three parts.

To be sure, the physical aspect of a patient can be maintained through technology, but that is only one aspect of the whole. More must be considered: Can the patient react socially in any way? Does he have any ability to respond spiritually? Can he show emotions? Can others respond to his emotions?

The Bible calls us to be much more than pro-life. We are called to be pro-human. The quality of our lives must reflect our manifold character as the crown of God's creation. If the social and spiritual aspects of a person are no longer functioning, then as Christians we must ask if this is the whole life that God intended for his image-bearers to have.

FOR PERSONAL PREPARATION

Think back to some experience you (or one of your family) have had with being ill and in a hospital. How did you react? If you were upset, what disturbed you about the situation—being away from home? Being treated as a patient (impersonal, inferior, ignorant)? The pain? The loss of control? The cost?

How did you deal with that upset? Did prayer, Bible reading, cards, visits by your pastor or elder, the presence of family, calls by friends help you? Did you learn anything important from that experience?

Chapter Three

THE CRISIS OF DEATH

Imagine that a physician has just told you that you have a terminal illness. How would you to react to that news?

Every day many people are told just that. According to United Nations' statistical estimates about 80 million deaths occur worldwide every year or about 153 every second. In the United States alone cancer causes 450,000 deaths each year, 5,000 every day, or four every minute.

These statistics are hard to ignore, but we do ignore them to the best of our ability. None of us likes to think about our own death. We even dislike using the words "death" or "died," preferring phrases like "passed away" or "went to be with the Lord." Yet we must confront the fact that we do not live in the land of the living but of the dying.

Death is part of living. Death gives meaning to human existence. It sets limits to our time on this earth and urges us to do something meaningful with that time. Death is a companion on our life's journey, reminding us not to put things off until tomorrow but to live our lives today.

Emotional Reactions to Dying

Those who know they are going to die soon go through five stages of emotional response—as do those close to them. There is a general pattern to these stages, and, although each person proceeds in his unique way, every dying person follows it to some degree. Some go through the stages in a textbook manner; others may skip one stage and come back to it later. Some pass from stage to stage very quickly; others, very slowly. The dying person may go through the stages in one way; the family may go through them in another.

Stage 1: Denial and Isolation

A person's initial reaction upon hearing the news that he will soon die is, "This can't be. You're reading the wrong report. You could not possibly be talking about me!" Trying desperately to receive better news, he may go to several physicians.

The loved ones of the dying person may not want to hear the terrible news either. Jesus' disciples, for example, refused to listen when he spoke of going to Jerusalem and dying there. Such denial often comes because of ambivalent feelings about death. We feel uncomfortable, knowing that some day it will be our turn. One of the benefits of funeral services is that they force us to come to grips with the fact that some day we will also die.

Denial is a human shock absorber in the time of tragedy. It temporarily desensitizes our emotions. Denial may display itself as displaced concerns—should we take a planned family vacation? Should we change the oil on the car? Will we like the new neighbors moving in next door? Denial may also lead to emotional detachment, but such frozen emotions must eventually thaw.

Stage 2: Anger

At this stage a person may ask, "Why me?" and even, "Why me, Lord? Terrible things are not supposed to happen to good people." The dying person may get angry with friends and relatives, with the doctor who delivered the bad news, or with anyone who happens along. He may express anger because he wants attention but feels people are pulling away from him. Anger is part of the normal process for any person dealing with imminent death although many Christians struggle with this emotion (see Appendix A).

Stage 3: Bargaining

Facing death, a Christian will often pray, "Lord, if you spare my life I will serve you more. I will be more conscious of my sin and spend more time in prayer." Or a loved one may bargain, "Lord, let him live until his child is born; that's the least you could do for him." Although this stage usually lasts a short time, it is very intense. The story of King Hezekiah provides a good example of this kind of bargaining (see Isa. 38).

Stage 4: Depression

If denial, anger, and bargaining have not worked, the person may conclude that nothing will change, and he becomes depressed. Depression has two parts: reactive depression, which focuses on the past, and preparatory depression, which focuses on impending losses. This is a time when the dying person and his loved ones need to pour out their sorrow, and, as in all the other stages, it is a time for others to listen with a nonjudgmental and caring attitude.

Stage 5: Acceptance

The dying person now comes to terms with what is going to happen. For most people this is a peaceful time when they become less active and talkative. At this stage Christians will pray, "Thy will be done." They know that dying, though unpleasant, is a passage to eternal glory. Even though they do not want to leave those they love, they are assured that what lies beyond is greater than anyone can describe.

The Tasks of Mourning

Even if the death was anticipated, those left behind must engage in the task of mourning. Jesus said, "Blessed are those who mourn, for they will be comforted" (Matt. 5:4). In our culture mourning is not an easy thing to do. The grieving person is supposed to be strong and brave even though it is unhealthy to repress normal emotional pain. Often mourners are left to their own resources at a time when those resources are most depleted.

We might suppose that in the church, at least, those who mourn are accepted and comforted, but often this is not so. Many Christian people suppress their grief because of subtle public pressure to be strong. Regrettably, they never complete the task of mourning, continue to live in the bondage of their grief, and are unable to live in victory and joy.

Even in the church we feel uncomfortable around grieving people. We are nervous, wondering when it will be our turn and helpless to know what to do or say. We often hide behind the idea that people of real faith do not have to grieve, especially not in public. But what grieving people need most, more than our words of comfort, is for us to allow them to express their feelings in our presence.

Emotional Responses of Grief

Just as dying people proceed through stages of emotional response, so their loved ones often follow a pattern of grieving.

Response 1: Shock, Denial, and Disbelief

While I was in seminary, I worked at a funeral home. One evening I was assisting the family of a man who had died unexpectedly of a heart attack. His teenage daughter had found him when she came home from school. On the night of visitation I noticed she never entered the room where her father's body lay. Recognizing that she was blocking out the fact of her father's death, an uncle asked me to help coax her into the viewing area. After most family members and visitors had gone home, I began to talk with her about the funeral arrangements. As we talked, I slowly walked toward the room where her father's body lay. Entering the room, I asked her if she approved of the way the flowers were arranged around the casket. For the first time she looked at the body. At that moment she fell to her knees and began to sob.

Shock and denial is a normal response to grief even if the death is expected. In high school I had a friend whose father was diagnosed as having a malignant brain tumor. We often talked about this, and she openly grieved about his impending death. After a year and a half of suffering, he died. I thought it strange that at the funeral my friend talked and joked with her friends as if she were at a party rather than her father's funeral.

About six weeks after the funeral, however, she came to my house very late at night. She had driven thirty minutes to get there. Knocking on my window, she asked me to come out and talk with her. Tears were pouring down her cheeks. "What is the matter?" I asked.

"My dad died!" she answered. Even though she had been prepared for his death for months, she had denied the actual fact for the past six weeks.

Response 2: Sadness, Depression, and Loneliness

After the reality of the death has set in, some people will lack the energy to do daily tasks. Nothing seems important to them. Nothing matters anymore. They may sit for hours looking at pictures of the deceased or just staring into space.

Response 3: Guilt

At this stage many "I-should-have" comments fill the conversation: "I should have taken him to the doctor earlier." "I should have been there when the doctor gave him the report."

The son of a family acquaintance was killed while riding a motorcycle purchased a week earlier. The parents struggled with the guilt of not having made their objections clearer. Guilt is a normal response when a person we love has died. We want desperately to turn back the clock and reverse the events that led to his death.

Response 4: Anger

Some grieving people may be angry at themselves because they feel guilty about the loved one's death, or they may be angry at the person who caused an accidental death. Anger at a physician, a pastor, or even God will often surface at this time. A natural response, anger should be accepted as part of grieving. (For a Christian understanding of anger see Appendix A.) Those who desire to comfort should listen with empathy and seek to help the mourner express, not repress, her anger.

Response 5: Restless Activity

A grieving person may have the energy to do many different tasks. She may, however, have difficulty returning to the daily routines she followed before her loved one died.

Response 6: Discontent with Life

A lack of vitality is characteristic of this stage. The grieving person feels as if life will never be the same again. The clouds have no silver lining, and the glass always looks half empty. Tasks seem to have no purpose because previously they were done in relationship with the deceased.

Response 7: Hope

When hope finally blossoms, life begins to seem good again. Joy in accomplishments is renewed. Now other people become interesting, and the bereaved person is able to look beyond personal problems to the concerns of others.

There is no set time for completing the tasks of mourning. To grieve the loss of someone close, such as a spouse, can take up to two years or more. People need to go at their own pace. The initial emotional responses may pass within the first months, but the other stages may take much longer. Some people will regress and go through a time of renewed anger or guilt. The important thing is that they gradually complete the task of grieving.

Unfortunately, some people become trapped in complicated or pathological grief. Distinguished from normal grief by the intensity or duration of the emotional response, pathological grief has four basic categories:

- Chronic grief—a person is stuck at one of the stages and can't seem to move on through the process.
- Delayed grief—a person doesn't allow himself to grieve the loss of a loved one, but another, minor loss sets off an inappropriate and severe grief reaction.
- Exaggerated grief—a normal reaction gets magnified into anger or even rage.
- Masked grief—a person has physical symptoms that are psychosomatic. At times bereaved people will experience symptoms of a disease that mimic the illness from which their loved one died.

Persons experiencing complicated grief need to see a counselor specially trained in grief therapy.

Attachment and Grief

In the beginning God saw that it was not good for man to be alone and so made woman. Thus he created us to be relational creatures, to make attachments.

If we do make attachments, however, we are vulnerable to loss. We become anxious when someone to whom we are attached is unaccountably missing. For example, when a mother realizes that her toddler is no longer in view, she is immediately concerned. When a child, who has been playing contentedly, sees that his parent has left the room, he will either cry or go to look for him.

One counselor has commented on how necessary it is for the Christian community to form attachments and thus, in times of trouble, to grieve with and for each other:

> Religion has traditionally encouraged people to care, to get involved, and "to love your neighbor." By so doing pastors are implicitly asking people to grieve as well. We should be clear about that. Grief is an inevitable part of love. The more we ask parishioners "to care," the more we are asking them to be willing to grieve. One cannot truly care without being hurt. . . . If we wish people to be "lovers" and caregivers, then we, as pastors, must help them learn how to grieve. Grief is a part of love (Wolfelt, 1988, p.16).

Studies of bonding disruptions between young children and parents have shown that there is a three-phase, grief-related pattern of protest, despair, and detachment. Separate a child from a parent and initially there will be tears of protest; the child hopes the expression of anguish will stop the parent from leaving. When the reality hits that the parent is not going to return immediately, the child withdraws into despair. If the separation continues for a long time, the child will, in a sense, forget about the parent and become detached. This same pattern can be observed in grieving people.

Even as infants we are able to form a mental image of a person to whom we have become attached. In that person's absence we maintain this internal image. The more the loved one is in our presence the more secure is the internal image. When the loved one dies—the ultimate bonding disruption—we experience the loss of part of ourselves, thus the frequent comment of the newly bereaved, "I feel as if a part of me died with him." In a real sense this statement is true because that person has not only lost her loved one, she has also lost the internal image of the other within herself.

The process of grieving necessarily involves the detaching of ourselves from the person to whom we have been so attached. Because one's internal image of the other person is so much a part of that attachment, a grieving person may engage in construct-retention. For a period of time the mourner will block out the reality of death by retaining a strong internal image of the deceased. The length of time that construct-retention lasts will vary according to whether the death was anticipated and whether the loving relationship was long or short. A widow who had been married for fifty years may vacillate between acknowledging the death of her spouse and talking about him as if he were still alive. This is not an abnormal or a pathological grief reaction.

Construct-replacement may also be part of the grieving process—the grieving person prematurely invests emotions toward the deceased in another person. But by avoiding the tasks of grieving in this way, a person places a burden both on herself and on the new person in the relationship, who often has the impossible task of living up to a ghost. Thus it is very unhealthy for a widowed person to marry again before the tasks of grieving have been completed.

The most healthy way to grieve is referred to as construct- reconciliation. The internal image of the deceased remains but begins to diminish through the grieving tasks. The deceased always remains an important part of the loved one's life but is part of many memories, with room left for other significant people.

Grieving Miscarriages and Stillbirths

When a woman miscarries, the first concern is for her physical condition; there is often inadequate concern about the parents' loss of a child. But the same processes of mourning that characterize all grieving will also be present in cases of stillbirth and miscarriage. It may be difficult for family and friends to sense the parents' grief; they have not seen the child and have not developed the same emotional bonds that the parents have had with the growing fetus.

People need to be more sensitive to the powerful emotions the family is experiencing during this time of loss. Too often medical personnel view miscarriage as a loss of tissue rather than a loss of life. One bereaved mother said to me, "My emotional pain over the miscarriage was made worse when the doctor said, 'I'll just clean up this mess inside you a moment, and then you'll begin to feel better.' "

Guilt may also be involved. The mother may feel that her actions resulted in the miscarriage. Perhaps she should not have exercised; perhaps she should have eaten more nutritiously; perhaps she should have stopped smoking. Such guilt could cause sexual dysfunction for a time.

The father generally feels powerless, and his attempts to be strong and supportive may be misinterpreted by his wife as being uncaring. At this time he may try to console himself and his wife by talking about conceiving another child. But it is an error to minimize the loss by focusing on the future possibility of other children.

Some couples may wish to see the fetus. Others may wish to hold a private memorial service. How the grief is expressed is not as important as the fact that the loss is acknowledged and grieved. The community should be supportive of whatever grieving the couple needs to pursue.

The greatest emotional danger for the grieving couple is to attempt to avoid grief by quickly becoming pregnant again. This is a form of construct-replacement that may have devastating consequences not only for the parents but for a child who begins life by replacing the memories, hopes, and losses surrounding a miscarried sibling.

Children and Grief

Adults must remember that the capacity to grieve depends not on one's ability to understand but on one's ability to feel. Any child who is able to love is able to grieve.

Because of their limited sense of time and space, however, young children cannot comprehend the total meaning of death. And grieving normally takes longer for them than for adults. They don't always understand that death is permanent, nor do they understand the need to release the strong emotional ties they had to the deceased.

Observing a child who has lost a loved one, some conclude that children do not grieve or are little affected by death. Experience shows, however, that children express grief through behavior rather than words.

The denial process for children is usually long and intense. At first they may act as if nothing has happened. The younger the child the more he will try to suppress the fact of death. Fantasies about the person returning from the dead may continue for up to a week for a child over the age of five and last much longer for a child under five.

Once the loss is accepted, a child may begin to act out scenes that involve the deceased loved one. Acting out is a healthy response, which enables the child to come to grips with the loss. The game "Ring around the rosy, pockets full of posies" was created by children during the Middle Ages as a way of dealing with deaths caused by the plague.

At first a child may reconstruct happy scenes, but after a time they may be sad. One mother was concerned because her child acted out the funeral of his father—he would line up three chairs; on one was the preacher, on another the funeral director, and on the third a person lying stiff. But again, this is a normal, healthy response for a young child who has faced death.

Guilt also comes into play in a child's grieving process and is stronger than that in an adult's. A child will often believe that the loved one's death was caused by his wishing it or by his doing or saying something bad. Adults need to help the child express these feelings of guilt and to give assurance that he was in no way responsible for the death.

During the grieving process a child's behavior may change. Those five years of age and younger may regress—wetting their pants or reverting to baby talk. School-age children may have psychosomatic stomachaches or headaches, or they may become very clinging or aggressive. Later, these children may become delinquent or do poorly in school. Generally, adults who lost a parent early in life tend to be more prone to depression and insecurity.

If a member of the family is terminally ill, children should not only be told but also helped to understand the dying process. And if death occurs, children should be given the news immediately. To be sent away after a death in the family may cause children to panic and to wonder if they will be allowed to return; such separation only adds to the guilt they already feel.

Children should also be included as much as possible in the funeral arrangements and, on the day of the funeral, given some task to help them feel useful and part of the family. Attendance at the funeral should be left up the children, after parents have explained what will be happening there.

When a death occurs in the family, it is also a time to talk about faith with children. It is best not to use phrases like, "The Lord took Daddy to live in heaven." That may cause the children to think of God as a cruel person. Rather, an adult should emphasize that God loved us so much he sent Jesus, who rose from the dead so that believers will live forever with him. Adults should also stress that the loved one is alive and will be seen again in heaven. The best advice is to be open and honest with children and to show feelings of grief and sadness.

FOR PERSONAL PREPARATION

Imagine that your physician had just informed you that you were terminally ill. How do you think you would react to this devastating news? Who would you turn to for comfort and counsel? How would this news change your relationships with other people? Would you tend to keep it secret from the church or tell everyone and ask for their prayers? Think about these questions for a bit.

Chapter Four

THE CRISIS OF DEPRESSION

I thought I was dying of some dread disease. My whole body hurt. Tylenol was my bread of life. At night I tossed and turned, and in the morning I couldn't move. I would go to my office and sit for hours staring at my books. Preparing two sermons a week seemed like climbing Mt. Everest.

One day I opened the mail and read a news sheet put out by our church's home missions department. The third box in the right-hand column read, "Ten Signs of Burnout and Depression." I perused each item with interest. I'd never had a higher batting average in my life. I began to cry. I was not dying! I was burned out and depressed.

Some of you might be thinking, "What a depressing subject." We live in a culture that stresses the importance of appearing alive and energetic. Our mottoes are "go-for-the-gusto," "party-hardy," "live-for-the-moment," and "shop-until-you-drop." In fact, however, among those who gather to worship on an average Sunday morning, ten to twenty percent suffer from some form of depression.

Depression has been called "the common cold of the mind." It may appear when someone is facing a crisis or when nothing out of the ordinary seems to be happening. Mental health experts estimate that one in every ten people in our country suffers from depression, and one in eight will require treatment. An estimated four to eight million people are so depressed that they cannot work effectively.

No One Is Immune

Depression is no respecter of persons. It's an equal opportunity affliction. Men and women, young and old, rich and poor, successful and unsuccessful—all are affected by depression. It's not true, as some think, that creative and sensitive people or those often in the spotlight—artists, movie stars, and politicians—are more prone to depression than the rest of us.

Certain subgroups are, however, more at risk. Overwhelming research shows a higher rate of depression in women than in men and in younger (18-44 years of age) rather than older adults. However, as our life span has lengthened, the elderly are showing more symptoms. Rates are also higher for separated and divorced persons than for those currently married or never married and for single rather than married persons. Studies also show that symptoms of depression are significantly higher in persons of lower income levels.

Over the past ten years understanding of the genetic factors that cause depression has grown tremendously. Compelling evidence now exists that hereditary factors can predispose a person to various types of depressive disorders.

The Causes of Depression

Why do people get depressed? Innumerable reasons exist, but the following are a number of possible causes.

1. *Past emotional deprivation*
    When a person is deprived of love and tender care as a child, mistrust, anger, and resentment will often build and result in depression during early adulthood.

2. *Improper food and rest*
    Lack of regular meals or sufficient sleep cheats our bodies of the sustenance they need to function properly. Scripture tells us we should take care of ourselves. Paul calls our bodies temples of the Holy Spirit; we need to make a good home for the Spirit of God.

3. *Reaction to medication*
    Medication often alters body chemistry. Depression can be a side effect of medicine used to control blood pressure or to treat other physical problems.

4. *Bodily systems gone awry*
    Our endocrine system includes various glands that pump hormones into our bloodstream. Imbalance of hormonal levels can result in mood alterations and depression.

5. *Anger turned inward*
    Repressed anger is a common cause of depression. As discussed in the previous chapter, Christians have often struggled with anger, assuming it should not be expressed. But it is very important to acknowledge, accept, and then deal with our anger in appropriate ways. Anger left to fester is depression waiting to happen.

6. *Grief*
   Grief-induced depression is normal and will usually pass as a person completes the tasks of grieving.

7. *Excessive self-pity*
   Most of us feel sorry for ourselves from time to time; that's normal. But wallowing in it is an invitation to depression.

8. *Behavior contrary to moral standards*
   A Christian involved in an adulterous affair or an unethical business practice or one who is not dealing with his children in a proper manner is susceptible to depression. Whenever our behavior violates scriptural teaching and we become depressed, we can honestly say that sin is the cause of our depression.

9. *Success*
   A person may expend so much physical and emotional energy trying to attain her goals that she becomes exhausted and depleted. Another person may feel inadequate in his new position. Someone else may have worked so hard to reach the top but now finds it unfulfilling. All these scenarios are fertile ground for depression.

10. *The pressure of perfectionism*
    Having excessively high expectations is a sure way to invite depression. It's impossible to be perfect in this life! In attempting to reach perfection a person will inevitably hit obstacle after obstacle and end up at a brick wall. Only Christ can be perfect. Our human lack of perfection is why he came to earth to redeem us. Our calling is to discover God's gifts and use them to the best of our ability and to his glory. Perfectionism aims at using our own gifts to our own glory.

Depression afflicts a variety of people for a variety of reasons. It's not abnormal or a sin to suffer depression. In some situations it may be a blessing, even a gift from God. Depression is a scream, a shrill message announcing neglect in some area of life. It's a warning of deep water ahead, a protective device that can give a person time to recover from stress.

Does Anyone Know What I'm Going Through?

A depressed person feels hopeless, despairing, gloomy, sad, and apathetic. Life seems to be moving toward deadness and emptiness. Changes in physical activities, such as eating, sleeping, and sexual functioning, may occur. Some people lose interest in food; others overeat. Some sleep constantly; others can't sleep at all. Inability to perform sexually may intensify feelings of worthlessness. Various physical aches and pains may be present.

A depressed person usually behaves in a way that reinforces the depression. He may lose perspective and develop a negative pattern of thinking about all of life. Aaron Beck of the University of Pennsylvania describes this phenomena as a "cognitive triad."

1. *A negative view of one's surroundings*
   Inner feelings affect whether a person views his surroundings in either a positive or negative light. For a depressed person all experiences are viewed negatively. Life becomes filled with obstacles and burdens. The glass is half empty instead of half full. The grass is always greener on the other side of the fence. And as negative thoughts build, depression is reinforced.

2. *A negative view of self*
   The way in which a depressed person sees life leads him to interpret all experiences, even neutral ones, as negative commentary on himself. For example, if someone forgets to return a phone call, he may interpret that action to mean the caller no longer wishes to be a friend. Neutral attitudes are seen as rejections, and neutral comments as hostile remarks. Everything appears to him in a way that fits into his previously drawn negative conclusions. Defeat is expected. He regards himself as deficient, inadequate, and unworthy.

3. *A negative view of the future*
   Because a depressed person interprets all experiences negatively, he will automatically feel that the future will be negative as well.

Results of this pattern of negative thinking are predictably tragic. The depressive mood paralyzes people, making it impossible for them to break the grip of negative thoughts. Caring little for themselves, they become increasingly dependent on others for their basic needs. And since all activities and relationships contribute to the pain, they seek escape through avoidance and sometimes suicide.

How does one break this negative thinking pattern? A variety of techniques are designed to help a person caught in this trap. But because such a pattern is fueled by a negative view of life, that first needs to be counteracted.

The Bible presents us with a wonderful perspective for living. Events in the world are not controlled by chance or by Satan. Jesus Christ rules the world and is working to fulfill his glorious kingdom. Because Christ loves us and empowers us with the Holy Spirit, we can view ourselves in a healthy way. For a Christian the future is glorious. We look forward to heaven but also to living now in Christ's kingdom. We receive spiritual gifts to use for Christ's glory every day—the fellowship of loving people to care for us and the assurance of rich blessings as we serve him.

Loss and Change

A real or perceived loss is often the cause of depression. Losses threaten our sense of stability, security, and well-being. The more sudden the loss, the more out of control the person will feel and the quicker and more severe the depression. The following losses may trigger a depression.

1. *Abstract losses*
   Loss of self-respect, love, hope, and ambition are abstract losses. When a person is passed by for a promotion, he not only loses the position and the income but also some self-respect and hope.

2. *Concrete losses*
   Losses a person can feel and see, such as losing a home, a car, a child, or an heirloom, are tangible or concrete losses.

3. *Imagined losses*
   A person may imagine that someone doesn't like him anymore or that other people are talking behind his back. These perceptions are often not based on fact.

4. *Threatened losses*
   These losses are the most difficult to deal with because they have not yet occurred, but there is a real possibility they will happen. Examples include such things as waiting for the results of a biopsy or the outcome of an important exam. A feeling of powerlessness in the face of threatened losses can result in depression.

Changes and transitions in life can also cause depression. When roles change, our beliefs, values, and assumptions may be challenged. If a number of changes occur at one time, a person may feel a loss of control over his life.

People often fear the loss of youth and the physical changes that result. Turning forty, a woman may become depressed because she fears she is no longer attractive, or a man, because he has lost his physical prowess. A mid-life crisis and subsequent depression can result when people face their own mortality and ask, "Is this all there is?" Depression is also common at retirement with the realization that one has passed into the final stage of life.

Depression and Stress

"Stress" is catchword for everyday tensions and pressures. In recent years it has come to dominate many of our discussions. A person may play golf on Friday morning and list this on a weekly calendar as "stress management exercise."

But if not properly dealt with, stress can upset our equilibrium and lead to depression. Our bodies have a sophisticated defense system that helps us cope with life's threats and challenges. When we feel pressure, they quickly mobilize for "fight or flight." Stress floods our bodies with adrenaline, a substance that disrupts normal functioning and creates a heightened sense of arousal. A stressed person is like a stretched rubber band. When the pressure is released, the rubber band returns to normal. But if it is stretched too far or too often, it begins to lose its elasticity and may eventually break.

Some stress is good—we need a certain amount of pressure and stimulation to keep us moving. Stress becomes bad when it is too much, too soon, or never relieved. Bad stress may cause long-term psychological and physical erosion and depression.

Not everyone's stress point is the same. Boredom, lack of meaning in life, or lack of challenge at work can produce stress in some people. For others the fast pace of life can be stressful. Children grow up in a hurry in contemporary society, and this pace continues into adulthood. Television, movies, and advertisements teach us to want everything, right now!

An excessive workload can also create pressure. Most of us take on too many activities and get involved in too many projects—even in our church life. So many opportunities for service are available in the church, school, and community that we often are running from the time we get up until we go to bed at night. This harried pace will not only wear us out but can lead to depression.

Certain stress points are unique to women while others are unique to men. For women stress often arises from physiological changes that occur as they age or from the emotional pressure of being a woman in a man's world.

For men the primary stress point is the issue of control. Men often can't handle feelings of dependency and vulnerability. They may feel uncomfortable sitting in the passenger seat of a car or waiting in line at a restaurant or movie; they are more likely to become angry at delay due to road construction or "stupid" drivers. Men also tend to dread funerals and will cancel counseling sessions or put off dental appointments more quickly than women will. They are leery of situations in which they have to put themselves in other people's hands.

Depression in Children

Children's depression is often hidden. Even if their children are chronically unhappy, parents typically deny the fact. Depressed children may just appear to be sad. They may not complain or even be aware of being depressed, but their behavior will show it. They may sit in their rooms, doing nothing for long periods of time.

Parents may attribute this listlessness to sickness or boredom. Often they look for physical symptoms and, indeed, may find some; headaches, stomachaches, and sleeping or eating disorders can blur the presence of depression.

In addition to having negative self-concepts and feelings of worthless-ness, depressed children tend to feel rejected or unloved. A disappointment may cause them to withdraw. Unfortunately, depression is the number one psychological problem among girls ten to fifteen years of age. It is often caused by low self-esteem connected with an obsession about weight. Our culture clearly states that only the thin are acceptable.

Irritability and a low frustration tolerance may be seen in some depressed children. Others may exhibit the opposite behavior, clowning around and provoking people. Such actions may occur even at a time of achievement because these children find it difficult to handle anything positive.

Because of their limited life experience, children do not experience or express depression in the same way as adults do. It may appear as rebellion, negativity, or anger. For example, a child's depression brought upon by a divorce in the family may manifest itself as bed-wetting, fighting with siblings, clinging to parents, failing in school, and exaggerated story-telling.

The causes of depression in children are essentially the same as in adults, but children may also become depressed because one of the significant adults in their lives is depressed. A counselor can help children climb out of depressive states by identifying the losses they have experienced.

How to Escape Depression

How long does a bout of serious depression last? Aaron Beck, whose findings about depression were discussed earlier, says that such an episode generally bottoms out within three weeks. Persons with prolonged depression usually seek help from either a family member, a physician, or a counselor. The good news is that there is a ninety-five percent recovery rate. In many cases depression goes away without professional help but, if needed, such help is readily available.

While depressed, people often do things they later regret; thus, they should avoid making any important decisions during this time. Failing to address the problem can only compound it, perhaps lead to chronic depression and, in some very sad situations, even to suicide.

A first step for the depressed person should always be a complete physical exam to discover whether a physical problem exists. Secondly, the person should examine his lifestyle from both a moral and a practical perspective to see whether that is the source of the problem. Third, it is important to stay active. Cutting oneself off from friends and family will only add to depressive feelings. Routines should be adjusted to include proper rest, nutrition, and regular exercise. Fourth, a person suffering from depression should always tell his loved ones. Letting out the hurt, anger, and feelings of loss will put things into proper perspective and allow others to help him understand what is happening.

Loved ones can also help by attempting to understand what the depressed person is going through. Saying "Snap out of this terrible mood you are in" will not help. The depressed person is not just in a bad mood; he feels as if he is down in a deep pit, which is dark, cold, isolated, and frighteningly lonely. On all sides are rocky, muddy walls, with no solid footholds to provide a way to climb out. He is totally helpless, resigned to days of darkness, with no means of escape (see Ps. 40:1-2).

Loved ones must also pray for both understanding and patience, not only for the depressed person but for themselves as well and receive guidance from a pastor or friend. If at first offers of help are rejected, they must keep trying. Persistence and unceasing encouragement is the ladder that may help the person climb out of his pit. A Scripture verse to cling to when one is in this situation is Isaiah 40:28-31. If, however, the depression does not lift, it is most important that the depressed person receive counseling.

FOR PERSONAL PREPARATION

Ask yourself the following questions, thinking carefully about each question and your own answer to it.

- Are you a perfectionist? When you think and talk about yourself, are you usually critical or complimentary? Do you like yourself?
- What causes the greatest stress for you?
- How do you respond to stress? By fight or flight?
- When did you last feel depressed? What was the cause? What losses did you experience with that depression?

Chapter Five

THE CRISIS OF SUBSTANCE ABUSE

I used to live in the central valley of California, an area that grows almost every fruit and vegetable known to man. Driving through the countryside, I would pass almond and walnut orchards and grape vineyards. Ernest and Julio Gallo lived just down the road, and their company produced an abundance of wine.

Because of the close proximity of wineries the matter of drinking alcohol was often discussed. Whenever it was, I would hear the following comments:

- "There is nothing wrong with a little drinking."
- " 'All things in moderation,' that's the Calvinist motto."
- "Talk against drinking just invites teenagers to rebel."
- "The wine business employs a lot of people in this area."
- "Alcohol need not become a problem for anybody; it's a choice each person makes."

In the privacy of the pastor's office, however, I heard:

- "The anger, yelling, and name-calling usually start at night after my husband has been drinking."

Of all the chapters in this study, this one is probably the most controversial—talking about the causes of substance abuse makes many of us defensive. Right now you may be thinking, "Talk to me about illness or death but don't talk about my use of alcohol. I'm doing fine, thank you." If you are discussing these chapters weekly with others, you may even be tempted to skip this one. Let me say a few things, however, that may deter you.

On the subject of substance abuse the United States national statistics are ominous. In 1988 it was reported that twenty-five percent of the teen population and fifty-five percent of adults use alcohol on a regular basis.

One in every ten adults is an alcoholic. In fifty percent of all traffic fatalities, seventy percent of all drownings, and thirty percent of all suicides, alcohol is a factor. Mental health professionals are telling us that alcohol abuse is involved in an astonishingly high percentage of divorces, sexual assaults, and child or spousal abuse cases.

Drug abuse in this country seems to be leveling off, but the reports still aren't good. Currently, six percent of teens use marijuana and 900,000 use cocaine on a regular basis. About seven million adults regularly use marijuana and two million use cocaine.

These statistics are hard to ignore. But we do ignore them to the best of our ability. We may optimistically cry, "I'll never become an alcoholic or drug abuser"; but this sentiment was also voiced by all those who make up the previous statistics.

The crisis of substance abuse is a tragedy that affects our nations, our cities, our churches, and our families. In this chapter we will learn how a person becomes a substance abuser, how this abuse affects his life, and how he can receive treatment. In the next chapter we will consider how substance abuse affects the abuser's family. We will deal mainly with alcoholism because the issues involved are basically the same as with other forms of drug abuse and because alcohol abuse is more common among us.

The Spiral of Addiction

Stage 1: Social Drinking

All drinking starts out as social drinking. Many of us drink a little alcohol with meals or as a relaxer before going to bed. Alcohol may also be part of our entertaining and socializing.

For most of us the first encounter with alcohol came during our high school days. What sort of experience that was depended on many things—the type of alcohol, its purity, its quantity, and the situation of our lives at that time. Was the drinking done at a party or during a crisis? Did it occur when the person who was drinking was happy or depressed? If the experience was good, if drinking made him feel more confident or helped him forget his troubles, then the person learned an indelible lesson—chemicals can change how you feel! The greater the mood swing, the greater the lesson learned.

For most teens, early experience with alcohol begins a lifetime pattern of social drinking. But for every ten teens who experiment with alcohol, at least one has taken the first step toward alcoholism.

Which of these young people will become alcoholics? Not even physicians, psychologists, or counselors can predict that with any reliability. Research to uncover what constitutes an alcoholism-prone personality has been inconclusive. What we do know is that those with the greatest perceived stress and the fewest effective ways of dealing with it are the most vulnerable.

In the last chapter we talked about the relationship between stress and depression. Attempting to avoid or deal with depression, some people try to drown their worries. But in our high-stress society, mixing alcohol and stress is like pouring oil into water.

Young drinkers learn quickly that alcohol temporarily eases emotional pain. But learning also takes place on another level. Their bodies discover that a given chemical relieves certain unpleasant sensations. That kind of learning is hard to erase.

In time many people move from learning the effects of alcohol to seeking those effects whenever they want a mood change. This pattern of behavior is still considered to be social drinking and is common in today's stressful living. We have often heard someone say, "What a day! Let's have a drink!" One drink may lead to three or four, or five or six. The evening may end in intoxication, and the morning may begin with a hangover. Many people can drink and stay at the level of never getting drunk—or only occasionally getting drunk—and never have further complications. But many others move on to worse situations.

Drinkers who are on the road to alcoholism will gradually, over months and years, consume larger quantities of alcohol and do so more often. Their drinking may not be excessive enough to attract much attention, especially if alcohol use is a normal part of their social life. At this stage we may hear comments like, "Harry just had a few too many at the party last night, but he doesn't have a problem."

This laid-back attitude toward public drunkenness is common even within the church community. I remember a man in his late fifties who was forced to go into alcohol treatment. After this fact became public knowledge, an elder told me that he recalled many times at private parties in the homes of church members when this man had been drunk. But nobody thought the man had a "problem."

Many people wrongly assume that alcoholism is only a chemical addiction. But long before a physical addiction becomes evident, an emotional dependency may be present. Individuals may be using alcohol as a way of dealing with life pressures, as a "pick-me-up" or a "relaxer." What they don't understand is that alcohol has become valuable to them and that they are as emotionally dependent on it as a toddler is on her blanket.

Let me give you an example. When relaxing at night in my chair, I like a nice cold root beer. But root beer does not have a value in my life. If there is none in the house, I don't run out to buy some; I don't become irritable, yell at my wife, kick the dog, or hit the kids. It's nice to have, but I can take it or leave it.

When alcohol takes on value in someone's life, however, no matter how little that value is, then that person has become emotionally dependent on it. Instead of dealing with life's challenges with maturity, alcohol abusers seek a crutch. Such a dependency on alcohol begins to produce emotional responses and reactions that will affect all their relationships in a negative way.

Alcohol affects more than one's mood. While the mind is enjoying a good time, the body is slowly adapting its chemistry to this stranger, a visitor that can move in to stay. At some point the drinker begins to need to drink more to get the same "buzz." Exactly how and why the body acquires this increased tolerance has not been determined. Whatever the chemical explanation, one thing is certain—increased tolerance is an early warning sign to a social drinker that serious trouble lies ahead.

Stage 2: Blackouts

If the warning sign of increased tolerance goes unheeded and larger quantities of alcohol are consumed, sooner or later will come another warning sign—the first blackout. This is a chemically-induced amnesia that occurs with regular heavy use of either alcohol or other mood-altering drugs. At first a blackout may last only a minute or two. As dependency develops, however, entire evenings or even longer periods can be lost from memory.

Blackouts are frightening. They can cause problems that are embarrassing and costly because neither the substance abuser nor his companions may be aware that a blackout is happening. A person may talk and act normally, giving no signs of intoxication, but for the period of the blackout remember nothing. The drinker can make promises, hear class assignments, negotiate business deals, incur debts, and have no idea afterward that he has done so.

When I was in college, I drove a truck for a man who was a heavy drinker. One night while playing baseball, I jumped up on the center field fence to try to prevent a home run for the opposing team and cracked some ribs. After treatment at the hospital's emergency room, I called my boss to tell him I wouldn't be able to work for a few days. I hesitated calling him late at night because I thought he might not be sober. But he didn't sound drunk while we talked about what had happened; he asked how I was feeling and told me to take all the time I needed to get over the pain.

The next day, however, his son came knocking on my door, angrily asking why I hadn't come to work or, at least, called in sick. I told him I had talked to his father the night before, but my boss evidently was having a blackout and remembered nothing of the conversation.

Studies of alcoholism have not determined the exact moment when the social drinker crosses the invisible line to total dependency, but some experts believe that the occurrence of the first blackout is evidence that the drinker is "hooked." Now alcohol is no longer consumed as a beverage but as a drug, and drinking is no longer a matter of conviviality and pleasure but of need. The dependent becomes preoccupied with alcohol. Although aware that he drinks more than other people do, he may rationalize his behavior but still feel guilty. He may sneak drinks, and time and money once devoted to family and other responsibilities now goes for alcohol. Drinking that causes problems with spouse or boss increases the load of guilt and further erodes the person's self-worth.

Whereas at an earlier time the dependent imbibed to change his mood from normal to euphoric, at this stage, when emotional pain is great, the best he can hope for is a change from bad to normal. When a person drinks for relief rather than pleasure, it is a sign that he is in serious trouble with alcohol.

Stage 3: Loss of Control

The next downward turn in the spiral of addiction is loss of control. Until now, despite clear signs of a growing dependency, the drinker could still stop drinking when she chose to do so. Once loss of control sets in, that ability is gone. The drinker can still make a choice whether to take the first drink but, after one or two, is unable to stop.

Encountering pressure from family, friends, and employers, the dependent person may become angry and voice threats or become hurt and cry. For a while her attempts to end the drinking may seem to meet with success: many alcoholics "go on the wagon" during this time. But the ride is usually short. The pain in a dependent's life has become so great that it cries out for relief. She may go into a bar thinking she will have only a couple of drinks but stay past midnight, drinking heavily. It usually takes a long time for an alcoholic to admit that she is unable to have only a couple of drinks and that the only way to recover is by staying away from alcohol completely.

As soon as drinking begins to cause complications in her everyday life, the drinker calls on the time-honored defenses of denying, avoiding, blaming, and making excuses. But the criticisms get sharper, the shame over the frequent episodes of drunkenness become more intense, and the sense of failure over inability to stay sober becomes greater. The drinker feels guilt about neglecting spouse and family, lonely as friends become fewer and fewer, and frightened as her job situation deteriorates and debts mount. To admit her predicament would bring more pain than she could handle.

Psychological defenses come to dominate all the drinker's interactions with others. This behavior is so predictable that anyone slightly acquainted with alcoholism can quickly recognize it. The drinker will use blame, threats, charm, and boasting and will try to avoid threatening situations. Such tactics may temporarily silence the accusers without but not the harsh accuser within. In order to survive, the alcoholic turns off her painful feelings and keeps them turned off with more alcohol, burying them somewhere deep in the subconscious. Unfortunately, positive feelings like love and compassion get buried as well. Objective truth also must be repressed, so the alcoholic gets further and further out of touch with reality.

The alcoholic's life now revolves more and more around alcohol. She hoards and hides bottles, drops all friends except for drinking buddies, and loses all interest in outdoor activities. If the job is not already lost, the alcoholic may quit, giving many bogus reasons. No longer a matter of choice, drinking dominates her existence and makes it impossible for her to deal with other aspects of life.

Stage 4: Withdrawal

The next downward turn in the spiral of addiction occurs when the drinker demonstrates withdrawal symptoms—convulsions, hallucinations, delirium, delusions, and tremors. These symptoms signal a crisis that occurs when the concentration of alcohol in the blood drops from its usual high level.

The body is making a clear and dramatic statement that physical addiction is now complete. In order to live with the continuing presence of large quantities of alcohol, the cells have slowly adapted by incorporating the chemical into their metabolic script. Whereas once they could not function normally with alcohol in the blood, now they cannot function without it.

During my days as a truck driver, I worked with another driver who was an alcoholic. He had been drinking for about thirty years. I never felt uncomfortable working with him when he was drinking his usual amount, but if it was close to payday, and he didn't have the money for booze, I never knew what he was going to do next. He would have such bad tremors that it was dangerous to be around him when he was operating any piece of equipment. Unfortunately, both he and my boss died terrible deaths because of the total deterioration of their bodies from alcoholism.

A life-threatening experience like withdrawal may reactivate the alcoholic's old resolve to be sober. It may even be the crisis needed to make him willing to accept treatment. This crisis can be the best thing that could happen to an alcoholic. But unless he gets treatment and is highly motivated to change, the weeks or months following this health crisis will only be a brief pause in the long downward journey.

Stage 5: Chronic Alcoholism

At this, the last, stage in the spiral of addiction the alcoholic's behavior now meets with unanimous social rejection. The person experiences a complete deterioration of moral and ethical understanding and becomes a total embarrassment both to self and everyone around him.

The chronic alcoholic will often experience impaired thinking. About ten percent have complete alcoholic psychosis with persistent indefinable fears and tremors. The liver often becomes dysfunctional, and all psycho-motor abilities, such as winding a watch, are greatly impaired.

A few months before my former boss died, I visited him in the hospital. I will never forget that experience. He was nothing but skin and bones and had lost all his hair; his skin was very yellow. He lay on the bed in a fetal position enduring incredible pain. It took him a long time to remember who I was. After talking just a few moments, his mind would wander, and he would babble like a toddler, saying nothing I could understand. It was one of the saddest, most pathetic experiences of my life.

What Has the Substance Abuser Lost?

Let's take a moment to consider the magnitude of an alcoholic's losses. Keep in mind the millions of Americans, young and old, who are addicted to alcohol.

When the drinker first began to use alcohol socially, we can assume that even though he may have been immature, he was nevertheless a fairly whole person. From the initial state of relative wholeness, the drinker's personal potential begins to erode in a variety of areas.

Spiritually, the alcoholic can no longer decide what does or does not have value. This function is usurped by the chemical. Alcohol has become a valuable resource, something that helps him through the stresses of life and is a source of power for living. For a Christian it is a sin to use alcohol as a means of relief from life's stress. The apostle Paul says that we are not to be filled with wine but with the Holy Spirit (Eph. 5:18). Alcohol is a false power, a deception. It does not help us solve life's stresses but only helps us ignore them.

In fact, the alcohol itself causes many new stresses and conflicts. Alcohol is an easy way out. The Holy Spirit, however, is the most power-ful source of strength in the universe, and to be filled with the Spirit is to receive the wisdom and strength to deal with the worst of life's problems.

If the downward spiral continues and the person becomes addicted, alcohol changes from something that has value to something that is a value in itself. In time alcohol becomes the central value in life—it becomes God. Thus the alcoholic lives in violation of the first command-ment of the decalogue, which tells us not to have any other gods besides the Lord.

Usually the alcoholic will break ties to any church with which he may have been associated. He is uncomfortable with church members and feels both anger and shame because of the criticisms—spoken or silent, real or imagined—about his drinking. Many alcoholics will turn away from God as well because of a growing sense of guilt and unworthiness.

Volitionally, the alcoholic loses the power to make choices. This is a slow process. Long before actual addiction he may have become so accustomed to numbing any unpleasant feelings with a drink that he has lost the tolerance for emotional tensions. Any choice that might cause the slightest personal discomfort is avoided through drinking no matter how high a value the choice might have. The alcoholic will grieve over neglecting family but still disappoint family members again and again. As dependency grows, he will lose the ability even to choose how much he drinks; the chronic alcoholic has few choices about anything.

Emotionally, the alcoholic loses all potential. Whatever the personal pain that first made drinking attractive, this person may once have been happy, at least part of the time. While drinking, he was still in touch with personal feelings, whether pleasant or unpleasant. But as soon as social drinking became dependency, good feelings decreased while uncomfortable feelings developed, which made the original discomforts—the reason for first using alcohol—seem mild indeed.

In time the alcoholic comes to experience a whole catalog of painful human emotions: anger, fear, hostility, resentment, shame, guilt, worthlessness, remorse, and depression. When the burden of the painful emotions reaches a point beyond toleration, he will repress and turn off all feeling. Gradually the alcoholic is no longer aware of guilt and shame but becomes completely numb, no longer able to relate to others or events as a human, feeling person. In the later stages of addiction the alcoholic even loses the ability to repress negative emotions, and a realization of the true situation descends in a flood of desperation and despair.

Physically, the alcoholic also experiences major losses. Skills, such as the ability to play sports, to dance, and to play an instrument, slowly diminish. Because of lack of exercise and neglect of personal hygiene, personal appearance worsens. Sexual desire and satisfaction wane. General health deteriorates because alcohol affects the skin, heart, blood vessels, neurological system, and even destroys brain cells.

The potentials of the mind also suffer. At first glance the alcoholic may seem sharp-witted—able to alibi, con, charm, and bluff everyone. A person far down the road to dependency can still plan ahead cleverly: he may maintain a supply of alcohol, find money to pay for it, keep it hidden yet always within reach, manage to hold a job, and maintain a facade in the community.

I have a friend who ran a successful business for a long time while in a state of dependency. He had bottles hidden under trees on the routes he usually took to job sites. When he built a large, new home, he had hiding places for his alcohol drawn into the architectural plans.

However, the alcoholic's cleverness is an illusion. The defenses he builds to protect himself from criticism and from his own painful feelings give him a highly distorted picture of reality. Rationalization and denial block out the truth about other people and other situations. Blackouts are an insult to the mind. In advanced stages of alcoholism, the victim can suffer hallucinations, brain cell deterioration, and psychosis.

The social potential of the alcoholic's life also falls apart. At first drinking may make a person braver in public, but the more a person drinks the more strained his social relationships will become. The alcoholic will write people off as boring or resent their well-meaning suggestion for help and will often abandon good friends and begin to associate with others whose lives revolve around alcohol. At home, relationships with family will be stormy, cold, and tearful. Often alcoholism is the chief factor in a divorce.

Ultimately, alcohol destroys every aspect of what it means to be human. In fact, it can progress to the point that a person barely resembles an image-bearer of God.

Treatment for Substance Abuse

Alcoholism is a physical and emotional addiction, a disease. Still, if a person is going to gain victory over alcoholism or any substance abuse, he must first understand it as a spiritual problem and pose the question, "What power is going to help me through the stresses of this life—alcohol or the Holy Spirit?"

Even non-Christian counselors have been impressed with the fact that those in the despair of the late stages of chronic alcoholism have displayed religious desires. The feelings of guilt and unworthiness that persist throughout the long decline reveal that the spiritual side of the person is never destroyed. Much of the effectiveness of Alcoholics Anonymous lies in its call to renew or establish a relationship with a "Higher Power."

For the Christian that higher power is the Lord Jesus Christ. After a person has committed himself to dependance on Jesus alone through all of life's troubles, he can have great hope that all aspects of life may come to reflect the way God created him to live.

Anyone who has lost control of drinking should get professional help. Some may be able to quit "cold turkey," but unless such a person receives professional help, he will become what is known as a "dry drunk"—someone who no longer drinks but still displays the emotional responses of an alcoholic.

It is best, of course, if an alcoholic seeks help before he gets to the stage of chronic alcoholism. Unfortunately, in many cases help is only sought after the alcoholic has hit bottom. At this point the person has usually lost family, job, and any other positive social network, has no money and no legal way to get it, and may be living out in the street because no one will take him in. This may sound cruel, but it may be the best thing the family can do to get the person to come to grips with his problem (see chapter 6 for a discussion of the effects of substance abuse on the family).

Another way an alcoholic may be brought to the point of seeking help is through an "intervention"—when family and friends, with the help of a professional interventionist, confront the alcoholic with the cold, cruel facts of his life. By intervening, family and friends create a crisis for the person. Alcoholics Anonymous members call such an intervention a "high bottom."

The interventionist will help prepare family members and friends for their role in the confrontation. In the intervention the alcoholic is confronted by every significant person in his life—a very intimidating and powerful experience. Usually a suitcase has been packed with personal belongings, and the alcoholic is given a choice—go into treatment or hit the road. A friend of mine who is a recovering alcoholic went through just such an experience; he recounted that the intervention helped him to understand what General Lee must have felt when he surrendered to Grant at the end of the Civil War—he was forced to lay down his guns when everything inside told him to rally the troops and fight to the last man.

Entering a rehabilitation center for treatment, an alcoholic will first go through a time of detoxification. Under the supervision of doctors and nurses and usually lasting from seven to ten days, detoxification occurs when the alcoholic's body withdraws from the grip of alcohol in the bloodstream. After the body is clean, the mind also begins to clear. During the following thirty- to forty-day rehabilitation period the alcoholic explores why he became addicted and designs a new pattern for living that will keep him away from alcohol.

To stay sober, the recovering alcoholic will often need the support of Alcoholics Anonymous meetings. For the first couple of months, daily meetings may be needed, followed by several years of once-a-week meetings. A person who maintains sobriety for five years or more may only need the support of the AA meetings during difficult times or may go to support others.

There is always hope for the substance abuser. No one is beyond help unless the person is in the last stages of chronic alcoholism and unable to live in a world of reality.

But the best way to avoid the spiral of addiction is to stay away from social drinking. Alcoholism involves a spiritual battle. The devil wants us to dodge our problems or escape them through chemical flight. Alcohol provides a quick and easy solution, one that first seems a smart way out. But what appears to be good is actually the path of death. That is how the devil always works, masquerading as an angel of light.

Alcohol deceives us into destruction with the false conviction that we will never have a problem controlling its use. The Holy Spirit, on the other hand, provides a rich, lasting power to overcome the stresses and crises of this world, a power at the disposal of every believer who asks for it in true faith.

FOR PERSONAL PREPARATION

Give yourself the following private self-test. Try to be as honest as you can.

	Yes	No
1. Do you lose time from work due to drinking?	☐	☐
2. Is drinking making your home life unhappy?	☐	☐
3. Do you drink because you are shy with other people?	☐	☐
4. Is drinking affecting your reputation?	☐	☐
5. Have you felt remorse after drinking?	☐	☐
6. Have you gotten into financial difficulties as a result of drinking?	☐	☐
7. Do you turn to lower companions and an inferior environment when drinking?	☐	☐
8. Does your drinking make you careless about your family's welfare?	☐	☐
9. Has your ambition decreased since drinking?	☐	☐
10. Do you crave a drink at a definite time daily?	☐	☐
11. Do you want a drink the next morning?	☐	☐
12. Does drinking cause you difficulty in sleeping?	☐	☐
13. Has your efficiency decreased since drinking?	☐	☐
14. Is drinking jeopardizing your job or business?	☐	☐
15. Do you drink to escape from worries or troubles?	☐	☐
16. Do you drink alone?	☐	☐
17. Have you ever had a complete loss of memory as a result of drinking?	☐	☐
18. Has your physician ever treated you for drinking?	☐	☐
19. Do you drink to build up your self-confidence?	☐	☐
20. Have you ever been to a hospital or institution because of drinking?	☐	☐

After completing this test, turn to the next page and read the evaluation given there.

If you have answered YES to any one of the questions, there is a definite warning that **you may be alcoholic.**

If you have answered YES to any two, the chances are that **you are an alcoholic.**

If you have answered YES to three or more, **you are definitely an alcoholic.**

(The above test questions are used by John Hopkins University Hospital, Baltimore, MD, in deciding whether or not a patient is an alcoholic.)

Think about what this self-test may say about you or what it may say about some members of your family or some friends.

Chapter Six

THE CRISIS OF CO-DEPENDENCY

Even sadder than the tragedy of substance abuse, discussed in the last chapter, is the damage done to the many people close to the abuser—the good and loving people who make up the addicted person's family and friends.

The number of people in the United States chemically dependent, or in close relationship with an addicted person, is estimated to be 80 million or twenty-three percent of the population. These are the people we work with, play with, and go to church with, the people who run corporations, hold government positions, and control our judicial system.

Substance abuse and its consequent problems affect the family of the abuser as much as the abuser himself. Dependence upon alcohol or drugs becomes the main focus of daily life, and family members often become co-dependents in the vicious downward spiral of addiction.

Some have claimed that co-dependents are sicker than the abusers themselves. Although that is not generally true, they do experience the pain of the abuse as much as or more than the abuser without the anesthetizing effects of alcohol or drugs. Co-dependents often question their own sanity. Still, their denial of the real problem can be stronger and harder to break than the abuser's own denial.

Rules for an Alcoholic Family

The credo of a family in which there is substance abuse is simple: "Don't talk, don't trust, and don't feel."

Rule 1: Don't Talk

As the spiral of addiction spins downward, family problems increase. The abuser's behavior becomes more irrational, and, for the family, this becomes the normal way of life. In an emotionally healthy home, talk would focus on this odd behavior, but in the alcoholic family the spouse and children have learned, through subtle or not-so-subtle means, not to talk about the drinking problem.

At first there may be discussion of family problems, but alcoholism is never considered to be the cause underlying them. Safe problems, such as trouble between husband and wife or parents and children, may be discussed, but the drinking is never brought up. It is easier to invent problems than to deal with the real issue. Cause and result get switched around. The abuser rationalizes that his drinking is the result of the family's problems when, in fact, it is the cause. The family is caught in a web of denial.

Friends, fellow workers, and church members can also become co-dependents when they participate in the denial and follow the same "don't talk about the real problem" rule. They may rationalize the drinker's problems and switch cause and effect around just like everyone else involved.

Even though it's never discussed, the abuser's alcohol problem is the most important thing in the family's life, and everybody knows it. Every day is planned around it—the abuser is obsessed with maintaining his supply, and the family is obsessed with cutting it off.

The "don't talk" rule also includes maintaining the status quo in the family, and that enables the alcoholic to keep on drinking. In an alcoholic family a very strange thing happens: as the alcoholic loses more and more control of his life, he gains more and more control of the family's life. The abuser will do whatever has to be done—sometimes violently—and say whatever has to be said to maintain the appearance of normalcy, and other family members will do their part as well.

I once talked with a wife who continued to deny the seriousness of her husband's drinking problem. Grasping for any sign that her marital problem was improving, she told me that he had written her a note that read, "Thank you for being such a good mother and for keeping the house so clean." She was crushed when I pointed out that her husband was really saying, "Thank you for maintaining the status quo, so I can keep on with the way I am living."

Members of an alcoholic family don't even talk about the real problem among themselves. They believe if they ignore it, perhaps it won't hurt so much, perhaps it will just go away. Some children may think they're losing their sanity because nobody seems to see what they see. Still they often say nothing. Adult siblings often discover, long after they have moved away from home, that all saw the same problem in their family, but none talked about it.

Claudia Black, in her book *It Will Never Happen to Me,* tells of a thirteen-year-old boy who was home alone with his father. In a semiconscious state from drinking, the father fell, hit his head on the coffee table, and lay bleeding. Arriving home a few minutes later, the boy's mother and sister picked up the father and carried him to the bedroom. No one said a word about the incident.

If members of an alcoholic family don't talk about the real problem to each other, they certainly don't talk about it to outsiders. Many children fear that they will not be believed—how could anyone's family be that crazy? Or they may feel guilty, thinking they would be betraying their parents by talking about such a delicate family issue. Many find the problems so complex and confusing that they have a hard time verbalizing their pain. Confronted with a parent's drinking problem, a child will often deny it and defend the parent against all odds.

Rule 2: Don't Trust

Children raised in an alcoholic family have learned not to trust others with the real issues of their lives. They have also learned it is best not to trust that anyone will be there for them, emotionally or physically.

To develop trust, children need to be able to depend on parents to meet their physical and emotional needs. In an alcoholic family, parents simply are not consistently available to their children because they are drunk, physically absent, or mentally and emotionally preoccupied with alcohol or the alcoholic. Children cannot depend on their parents to be there when they get home from school, to prepare their meals, to pay the electric bill, to be sober at their birthday parties, or to remember promises made to them.

In the home a feeling of safety is also a prerequisite for trust to exist. Children need parents' friendly help, concern, and guidance. If alcohol is abused in their home, however, children often can't rely on parents to provide any of this safety. They will often tell stories of a drunken parent driving recklessly or of fires caused by drunken neglect. Their safety is also frequently jeopardized by verbal and physical abuse.

Security is seldom present for any length of time in a family struggling with alcoholism. The family may be forced to move often because the alcoholic father can't keep a job. For the child this means never establishing roots or close friendships. It means always being the new kid in school. Children in these situations often can't bring friends home to play for fear they will be harassed and embarrassed by their alcoholic parent. Honesty is another important element in maintaining trust. As the disease progresses, however, an alcoholic loses the ability to be honest. A parent will often give false information in a feeble effort to protect a child from reality. Tone of voice and body language, however, will lead the child into second-guessing about what is really happening. It is even more difficult for children to feel trust when certain incidents in the home are not discussed or are minimized, rationalized, or blatantly denied.

In an alcoholic family all the attention is focused on the alcoholic. Thus the children learn that when they have a problem it will be ignored; it's better to try to deal with the problem themselves or ignore it as everyone else does.

Rule 3: Don't Feel

Because he is in such emotional pain, the alcoholic can't handle the painful feelings within the family. As the one who makes the rules, the drinker requires that everyone's true feelings be hidden. As a result family communication is severely hampered. What remains tends to be rigid, distorted, and incomplete, with the messages bearing little resemblance to real facts and feelings. Listening to an alcoholic family converse is like hearing a group of robots report the daily news. No one really cares what the others are feeling as long as the appearance of normalcy is maintained.

The alcoholic's expressed feelings only hide true feelings:

- "If the kids would show a little responsibility about money, I wouldn't have to be so hard on them. [I'm worried that I'm going to lose my job.]"
- "If you were more affectionate, I wouldn't stay out late at night. [I know I'm not satisfying you; I'm not sure I could if I tried.]"
- "Why should I go to church? That new minister is only interested in money. [I'm no good. I can't face the minister or the congregation.]"

Often the false emotions expressed are the opposite of the underlying, true emotions. But ironically, as the following diagram shows, the alcoholic's behavior evokes the same underlying, painful feelings in family members.

Dependent's True Feeling	Dependent's Behavior	Family Members' Feelings
Guilt, Self-hatred	Blaming	Guilt, Self-hatred
Anger, Rage	Fear	Fear
Helplessness	Controlling others	Helplessness
Hurt	Abusiveness	Hurt
Rejection	Rejecting	Rejection
Low self-worth	Grandiosity	Low self-worth

The alcoholic family's "don't talk, don't trust, don't feel" rule teaches children it isn't safe to express their feelings. Eventually they learn to deny feelings because they don't trust that they will be validated by family members. Not perceiving others as resources, children of alcoholics tend to be lonely, to keep to themselves.

Kathy is a cheerleader for her high school's basketball team. One night her father came to a game noticeably drunk. Raised in a healthy family, Kathy would have been angry, embarrassed, and humiliated. But as a part of an alcoholic family, she didn't feel any of these emotions. She did what she had learned to do—she calmly took her father out of the gym before he hurt himself. Returning later, she showed no emotional reaction. She didn't mention the incident, and none of her friends did either. Kathy understood that letting her feelings take over when a situation like that occurred would only result in too much pain.

Children of alcoholics learn to build strong walls to avoid dealing with the reality that their world is in chaos. They learn never to ask questions like, "Why do my parents always embarrass me?" "Do they really love me?" "Are my parents going to get better?" "Are they going crazy?" "Am I going crazy?" It is frightening to ask such questions; it can be even more devastating to answer them.

Roles in an Alcoholic Family

The alcoholic does not go down the road to destruction by himself; everyone who loves him often helps to play out the drama of his life. Without them he would have had to face the consequences of his actions long before his dependency on drinking could develop into full-blown addiction.

Role 1: Chief Enabler

Even at a relatively early stage the drinker's behavior is becoming unhealthy, irresponsible, and antisocial. He rarely has to deal with the consequences, however, because out of compassion and understanding the people who love him, especially his family, help protect him from embarrassment and humiliation. They try to soften the blow by saying, "It's only happened a couple of times and probably will never happen again." This process is called enabling or co-dependency. Melody Beattie in her book *Co-dependent No More* describes a co-dependent person as "one who has let another person's behavior affect him or her and who is obsessed with controlling that person's behavior" (p. 37).

Why would anyone knowingly help a loved one destroy himself with alcohol? The answer is, of course, that such a choice is not knowingly made. Rather, the small daily choices that enable the alcoholic are made individually, under stress, and without clear understanding of the real effects on the course of the abuser's disease.

The chief enabler is the person most emotionally attached, usually the spouse. An enabling wife often responds out of a sincere, though misguided, sense of love and loyalty. Sometimes she may react out of shame, trying to protect her family's self-respect. And she may be motivated by fear that she and her children will share the unfortunate consequences of the abuser's behavior.

It is natural to want to protect and help the people we love. It is also natural to be affected by and react to the problems of people around us. As problems become more serious and remain unresolved, we react more intensely to them.

Co-dependents are reactionaries in the emotionally weak sense of the word. They overreact, they underreact, but rarely do they act. They react to their own problems, pains, and behaviors; more importantly, they react to the problems, pains, and behaviors of the abuser. Ultimately, the enabler has no control over her life either.

As the abuser's dependency on alcohol increases, the enabler spends all her time fixing things, trying to explain the problem to her children, and smoothing over embarrassing incidents with friends. She is constantly trying to keep ahead of the next potentially embarrassing situation.

For a long time she will excuse the dependent's problem as stress related—or create some other reason—but she will not attribute it to his drinking. Like her spouse she is caught in a web of denial.

Before long the enabler finds herself becoming both mother and father. She has to control the household, fix the plumbing, mow the lawn, wash the car, make most of the family decisions, and control the finances. She may have to get a job to support the family. People will look at the co-dependent and marvel at her talents and ambition, never recognizing her emotional pain.

What the enabler does not understand is that all her attempts to fix things only make the situation worse. She is preventing the crisis from happening that may offer the abuser and his family their only hope for a healthy home life. The abuser needs all his "crutches" pulled out from underneath him. He needs to hit bottom. A crisis is the best thing that could happen, painful at first but, like a disinfectant, necessary for healing.

Just as the alcoholic can find help through Alcoholics Anonymous, the enabler can also find support through Al-Anon. This organization helps co-dependents to understand that they are not alone in their grief and to find some stability even if their loved one keeps drinking. This stability comes when the enabler begins taking control of her own life. For many co-dependents discovering the true nature of the problem and their own enabling role can be a very difficult and painful process.

Christian women make great enablers. From their first day in Sunday school, they have been taught precisely those virtues that propel them to side with their abuser: covenant faithfulness, sacrificial love, compassion, forgiveness, and long-suffering. They have been taught to be submissive to their husbands, to be wholly dedicated to the well-being of marriage and family, to make sure husband and children are happy and respected. To do less is not merely a blow to self-esteem but a sin. In an alcoholic home, however, doing your duty and helping your loved one in any way you can is the path to disaster.

This is why it is often so hard for Christians to break the bondage of addiction. Whenever I talk to a spouse, a parent, or a grandparent about the steps needed to bring the abuser to the point of seeking help, they look at me with disgust. They don't understand how I, a pastor, could tell them, "You must say to your loved one: unless you stop drinking, you're no longer welcome at home." That sounds so cruel, so unloving, so unchristian.

The devil has us backed up against a wall when we deal with alcoholism. What I, as a pastor, need to say and what the co-dependents need to hear sounds so demonic, so selfish. One father told me, "We must reject your counsel and continue to love our child. As we love her and help her, she will see the error of her way." But this kind of love will only lead to more disappointment and pain. The abuser cannot respond to the parents' love in a way that will overcome the addiction. Rather, her physical and emotional dependence on alcohol will force her to take advantage of any love offered as a way to feed her addiction. Enablers need to realize that the one with whom they are dealing is not the person they love but the demon that controls her. Until the abuser stops drinking, family love must go in very different and unconventional directions. It must become what some have called "tough love."

Role 2: Responsible Child

The children of alcoholics are not always easy to spot. They are not all problem students in school or juvenile delinquents. The majority of them appear as if they come from normal, healthy families. But beneath the appearances differences abound.

In healthy families children learn roles that help them take on responsibilities and develop sound personalities. Children of alcoholics learn roles, too, but, these roles merely enable them to survive the chaos of their lives.

The oldest or only child in an alcoholic family will often take on the role of the responsible child or will become, what others appropriately call, the "family hero." This child is a resource in a family of few resources, the one who provides those moments of hope and pride that even the most desperate families experience. Ironically, the hero may also be the most difficult member of the family to reach with treatment.

As the alcoholic and the enabler become more and more preoccupied with drinking, the hero takes on the responsibilities of the home. She is the fixer who tries to bring stability, to correct imbalances, and to heal the family's pain. By doing this, she hopes to heal her own emotional pain as well.

The hero learns early that the best way to stay out of trouble is to be very, very good. A child in a healthy family also learns this lesson, but she knows she will be accepted even if she is not good. In an alcoholic family being good is the only way a child can be noticed or accepted. So the hero learns to bottle up negative feelings—those are sure to make someone angry—and to express positive feelings—those will win approval. The hero gives people what they want as a means to control the situation and to get what she wants.

Mature beyond her years, the responsible child attempts to take the place of the missing parent and the parent preoccupied with controlling the alcoholic. When her father gets drunk and starts hitting, she's the one who grabs the coats and the younger children and heads for the neighbors. This child makes sure that everyone gets up in the morning and off to school on time, washes the dishes, mows the lawn, and does the grocery shopping. One nine-year-old daughter of an alcoholic had a flow-chart across her bedroom wall marking what she needed to do each day to run the household.

The responsible child learns to set goals and carry them out. Knowing the impossibility of planning much past the present, she determines what can be accomplished and how it can be done on that day.

In school she is often a "straight A" student, respectful to adults, and capable of carrying responsibility beyond what is characteristic of her age. She is on the honor role and in the National Honors Society. The talk of the town and congregation as the one who can accomplish anything, she experiences success in a wide variety of areas far sooner than most people. But this is also someone who is dying inside, for the ultimate goal—achieving self-worth—is always beyond reach.

As an adult the responsible child continues these heroic efforts. The responsible lifestyle, which enabled survival as a child and aids survival as an adult, is often a point of pride. But changes occur as the hero moves on in years—increased anxiety, tension, and a feeling of alienation from other people.

Forced to grow up so fast, the responsible child is someone who never had time to be a child. When grown, she often has problems relaxing and seeing the humor in life, is rigid and lacks flexibility, and needs to feel in control. Relationships are always win-lose situations; she has trouble with intimacy because she is not able to communicate feelings, only facts.

Some adults, who were the responsible children in alcoholic homes, begin drinking as a way to relieve the tension in their lives. They may feel that it helps them respond to other people, and, in turn, others seem to respond better to them. So drinking becomes something that makes life good and livable. This may, however, be the beginning of the road to addiction for them.

Although she is often the toughest one to help, there is hope for the responsible child. Al-Ateen, a support group for teenage children of alcoholics, is designed to help teens develop emotionally healthy ways to deal with a parent's addiction. And Adult Children of Alcoholic (ACA) support groups bring healing to adults who grew up in alcoholic homes and are experiencing emotional and relational problems due to the rules and roles they have carried over into adult life.

Role 3: Adjuster

Another role in the alcoholic family, the adjuster, is usually taken by the second or middle child. This child finds it much easier to exist in the chaotic family situation by simply adjusting to whatever happens—not trying to prevent or alleviate it. The adjuster doesn't think about or react emotionally to the situation; whatever happens, when it happens, is simply handled in terms of the credo: "I can't do anything about it anyway."

The following are typical scenarios involving adjusters in alcoholic families: a young boy receives permission from his alcoholic father to play with a friend after lunch, but as he goes out the door, the father orders him to get back into the house. The son quietly calls his friend and makes an excuse about why he can't come over. A girl, whose alcoholic father never attends her piano recitals, simply rationalizes that he probably would have shown up drunk anyway. Both children find it easier to accept the facts and not attempt to do anything about them.

To an outsider the adjuster appears to be detached from the family; to the other children he may seem selfish, and to the parents, oblivious about what is going on. While the responsible child is very noticeable in the home, the adjusting child will play alone for hours in his room or spend most of his time outside the home playing with friends. Some call the adjuster the "lost child" because his way of dealing with problems is to "get lost." This child has learned that adjusting to any situation, either by compliance or absence, is the only way to be appreciated and accepted.

Claudia Black tells the story of a young girl who went to a ball game with her father. On the way home he stopped at the B. D. Tavern, a bar fifteen miles from home. Handing his daughter the car keys, he told her to drive home and have her mother pick him up later. Although she didn't know how to drive, the daughter didn't question her father's instructions but started the car and pointed it toward home. She ran in and out of several ditches and drove mostly on the shoulder but got home. Arriving there, she told her mother where her father was and when he wanted to be picked up and, saying nothing further, went up to her room and to bed.

Academically about average, the adjuster draws little attention of either a positive or negative kind at school. Somewhat detached from and outside of social circles, he plays with other students but never takes a leadership role.

This survival pattern usually continues into adult life. Adult adjusters find it difficult to take responsibility for or control of any situation. They may find it hard to stay in one place very long, hold down responsible jobs, or maintain stable or intimate relationships.

Adult adjusters often lack direction and feel that they have no control over their lives. But they do not examine their true feelings or easily allow others to help them. Alcohol can remove their feelings of inadequacy and give a false sense of power. When drinking, they discover options and choices of which they were previously unaware and find it easier to make decisions and to talk about the real issues. Alcohol helps them feel good about themselves, but it can easily become psychologically, if not physically, addicting.

Role 4: Placater

Yet another role that a child may take in an alcoholic family is as placater. This role is usually filled by the third child or one of the middle children. In every family there is usually one child who is most sensitive, whose feelings are most easily hurt, who is quickest to say, "Let's forgive and make up." In the alcoholic family the placater takes on this role because it's the best way to survive in the tension-filled environment.

The hero tries to fix things by being responsible, the adjuster by being compliant, and the placater by being the peacemaker. This child likes to make others feel better to lessen both her own and others' tensions and pain. If her mother and father are arguing, the placater will try to diminish the other children's fear. If a sibling is embarrassed by a drunken parent's behavior, this child will attempt to make them feel better. If a brother is angry because the father broke another promise, the placater will try to dispel that anger. This pattern may develop at a surprisingly young age. These sensitive characteristics are displayed at school as well. The placater is often well liked by both students and teachers.

Placaters play their role to avoid self-disclosure as well as to avoid seeing the reality of their situation and experiencing its pain. Accordingly, these children are highly skilled at diverting attention away from themselves and focusing it on the problems of others.

Like her counterparts in the alcoholic home, the placater's pattern of survival continues into later life. It is not unusual to find adult placaters in the helping professions. They seem to attract, and have a powerful desire to help, people with emotional problems. This may be a wonderful trait, but it can take its toll. Many adult placaters suffer from depression because they are unable either to fix the problems of the world or to face their own problems.

These people often feel lonely and apart. They lack equal relationships with others; unable to receive, they always give too much. In intimate relationships placaters find people who are takers and accept the emotional responsibility of fulfilling the other person.

Unfortunately, adult placaters, like others raised in homes in which substances were abused, often turn to alcohol for relief. They may believe that drinking helps them to talk more freely about themselves, to feel more self-worth, to become more assertive, and to feel a greater selfishness. It even helps them to become angry. Since drinking assists them to express the emotions that have been bottled up for a long time, it is easy to see how the spiral of addiction is never too far away for them.

Role 5: Scapegoat

The final role in an alcoholic family is what some call the "acting-out child" or the "scapegoat." Most children of alcoholics react in ways that avoid drawing attention to themselves or other family members, but the scapegoat is different. While others may be trying to fix things, the scapegoat tries to wreck them. While others are suppressing their anger, the scapegoat displays it in unpleasant ways. This child's delinquent behavior most adequately typifies the state of the family.

He is the only person who is acting, not simply reacting. He is the scapegoat because it is very easy for the family to blame this child and ignore the real problem of alcoholism.

These are the children that we more easily identify as the products of alcoholic homes. They begin acting out at an early age by hiding under the bed, refusing to get dressed, and running away from home. They are ones who drop out of school, get pregnant as minors, and flood our criminal justice system. They are found in drug treatment programs, halfway houses, foster homes, psychiatric hospitals, and, most tragically, in the county morgue. Unfortunately, thousands of acting-out children never receive any help. For those who do, the help often deals only with their behavior, not with the real problem of the alcoholic family system.

When grown, scapegoats will continue to experience conflicts. Through all of life they are often unable to interact with others in acceptable ways and to express their needs or have them met. As acting-out children they were always aware of their anger but seldom aware of other feelings. As adults this pattern continues. They will continue to gravitate to others who feel left out and worthless. They will seldom enjoy lasting intimate relationships because they don't know how to express intimacy.

Acting-out children usually begin experimenting with drugs and alcohol early in life. Many become addicts and alcoholics while they are teenagers. Unless there is intervention and treatment leading to recovery, these young adults often die premature deaths due to the rapid progression of the disease.

FOR PERSONAL PREPARATION

Take a close and careful look at your own family—either your family of origin or present family, either your nuclear or broader family. Ask yourself the following questions:

1. Can my family be characterized as dysfunctional (unhealthy) in any ways?

2. Did my family (or does it) display signs of co-dependency as described in this chapter?

3. Are there any members of my family who display addictive behaviors (related to abusiveness, gambling, work, spending, eating, athletic activity, etc.).

4. Is there a tendency for family members to take on some of the roles described in this chapter?

Chapter Seven

THE CRISIS OF DOMESTIC VIOLENCE

A symbol of safety, home is for many people a place of escape from the world's pressures and a haven of support from loving people. But for others—perhaps also for you—home is a place of pressure, of stress, of shame, because it is a place of violence.

Some of you may wonder—even be appalled—that this book, written for use in church circles, includes a chapter on domestic violence. But recent studies in many denominations show that battered women and abused children are also present in our churches. This horrible sin and the agony it causes may be hidden, but it does exist in all our congregations.

In 1990 I attended a seminar on crisis ministry at Fuller Theological Seminary. Three days of that seminar were devoted to domestic violence. As the professor was speaking, I tried to recall any incident of such violence in the eleven churches I had known, in the four in which I had served as pastor. I could not remember one single incident.

At the end of the three days the professor asked if we planned to pray for those who live in violent homes. All of us eagerly committed to doing so. Immediately she responded, "I must warn you. If you pray for battered women and children, they will hear you and perceive you as a new, understanding voice in the church. They will come to you. So be prepared."

When I returned to my congregation, I began to mention battered women and children in my public prayers. After a few months the professor's prediction came true. The battered, suffering people came to me. Fearfully, skeptically, and shamefully but, thank God, they did come and continue to come.

Why did they suffer so long? Why do many still suffer silently? What have we been doing in our churches that this abomination before God has existed and still exists?

Why Women Stay in Abusive Relationships

From the perspective of the Christian community it is understandable that women don't flee abusive relationships. For many centuries they have been taught that, as a result of the fall into sin, enduring abuse is their lot in life (see Appendix B for a historical review of such teaching).

In fact, saying that the Bible instructs women to be subject to their husbands, some pastors have even counseled women to stay in abusive homes. And they have informed those who have fled to women's shelters that, if they do not return home immediately, they will be excommunicated for breaking their marriage vows.

Women are often pressured to keep the family together at all costs. They are told to pray more fervently and have more faith. They are taught that if they suffer and pray, the Lord will teach them where they have failed, that such suffering will work for their own good and make them better witnesses for the Lord.

One woman, a lifelong member of the church, told me that every Mother's Day sermon gave her husband more ammunition to keep her in an abusive relationship that had lasted almost thirty years. Another woman, calling long distance, told me of the abuse she suffered as a child from her father, a pastor in our denomination. When she married, her father told her husband that it was now his responsibility to discipline her.

Until the early 1970s the stories told by abused women to psychologists and pastors were often dismissed as exaggerations, as tales of women who wanted to be treated roughly or who needed to be punished for some psychological reason. The myth was perpetuated that women stayed in abusive relations because they somehow liked them, needed them, wanted them, or deserved them.

A 1990 episode of the television program "L. A. Law" exposed this myth. It portrayed a woman, two years after a divorce, suing her husband in civil court because he had beaten her continually during the twelve years of their marriage. The husband's defense pointed out that he—not she—had initiated the divorce and that after their "fights" they often made love in which the wife seemed to be passionate. But the jury found the man guilty and awarded his wife a substantial sum. Abused women are not masochists who enjoy life on the rough side.

Reasons Why Women Stay

Women stay in abusive situations for a variety of reasons. The first relates to the platonic mind-body dualism (described in Appendix B) that has so influenced our western culture and has led to the social subordination of women.

When a man and woman marry, they come with many preconceived ideas about male and female roles. Women are expected to make marriage their central life focus, to be the caretakers of the home—tasks related to the body half of the mind-body dualism. A good wife keeps the house clean, cooks the meals, dresses the children, and sees to the physical, emotional, and sexual needs of her husband. A woman's identity is fashioned around her ability to create and maintain a successful marriage and raise happy, well-adjusted children. Even today, when women have vocations and interests outside the home, marriage and the tasks associated with motherhood are still considered their primary consideration.

In our culture the social expectations for men are quite different. A man's public identity and career are seen as primary, while his roles as husband and father are secondary. A man's success is measured by his ability to function in the public arena, to provide for his family, and to develop his individual potential to the fullest. Boys are taught that the home is not their chief place of concern but rather where they go to satisfy their physical and emotional needs.

In abusive situations, therefore, women are clearly at a psychological disadvantage. Furthermore, the verbal abuse that often accompanies physical beatings is very destructive to their self-esteem. Many women do not leave a relationship because they don't believe they are able to live on their own. Told over and over that they are stupid and that no one would put up with their inabilities as wife and mother, abused women soon come to believe this to be true.

Abused wives are also in a no-win financial situation. Many have never worked outside the home and lack the job skills needed to provide for themselves and their children. Economic facts bear this out. Homes headed by a single female parent are often at or below the poverty level. Three out of five working women earn less than $10,000 per year, and nearly two-thirds of all minimum-wage workers are women. In the first year after a divorce the woman's standard of living drops an average of seventy-three percent, while the man's increases forty-two percent.

Some women do not leave abusive relationships because they have no family support and no place to go. Others come from a long history of such situations and believe that an abusive home is better than no home at all. Some also believe that their children will be emotionally damaged if there is no man in the house.

What commonly keeps women in abusive relationships is fear. They are afraid that if they leave or seek help they will be beaten or killed. Their batterers daily threaten to kill them if they ever tell anyone, report the abuse to the police, or leave. These women have good reason to live in fear because many are severely injured or killed when they break the code of silence.

When their husbands start abusing the children as well, then abused women often take the final step of leaving and seeking help. Responding to their children's pain even though they may not have reacted to their own, they are moved to protect the children, and this action brings a ray of hope to the family.

The Make-up of a Batterer

Previously, the psychological response to a report of abuse was to assume that the violent person was mentally ill. Over the past twenty years, however, this view has changed. Reports indicate that only about ten percent of abusive incidents are caused by mental illness. The root cause of the remaining ninety percent lies in the structure of the family and the cultural, societal conditioning.

Everyone is born with a natural tendency to sin. Parents make rules and set limits to control this tendency in their children. Every child goes through what is referred to as "the terrible twos." This is a normal, developmental stage during which children selfishly see everything as belonging to themselves and the world as revolving around their own needs and wants. As they grow older, if they are being raised in a healthy environment, children learn to share and play with others. They learn that they cannot control the world but must respect other people. They also learn to give and to love in a way that serves others.

Lack of loving discipline and an environment that encourages a good sense of self-worth causes abusive persons to get stuck in the terrible twos. Growing up, they learn to view all relationships in terms of power and control. In a feeble attempt to build up their own low sense of self, abusers feel the need to control and belittle other people, especially those who are close to them.

In a healthy home self-sacrificing love is the center of all relationships. Each person works to create a safe environment in which everyone is nurtured, encouraged to be emotionally responsive, helped to be productive, and empowered to become the persons God created them to be. Through this love each one builds the self-esteem of the others.

In an abusive home, however, power and control are the driving forces in all the relationships. The abusers are oppressive, coercive, demanding, exploitative, and destructive. Abuse lowers the self-esteem of abusers as well as of the abused, making them incapable of becoming loving persons.

Abusive, violent men have a number of distinctive characteristics. First, they are unusually anxious about and have an exaggerated need to prove their masculinity. Some sociologists trace this need to the routine socialization of boys in our culture. Although they can be well educated, congenial in their public and professional lives, and pillars of church and community, at home violent men are brutal towards women. Insecure masculinity drives them to try to maintain a superior and controlling position in their private lives.

Second, violent men accept the cultural assumption that real men should be tough and in control of their emotions. As one counselor explains:

Boys don't learn to express their feelings, which makes it difficult to feel comfortable in intimate relationships. In intimate relationships you must be vulnerable. The men who batter say they want to be close to their wives, but it frightens them because in adulthood it evokes homophobic feelings; it is identified as womanly, which is so frightening. The men articulate this by saying, "That's for women" (Bussert, 1986, 44).

Although they may demonstrate verbal skills in their public and professional lives, abusive men have difficulty identifying and expressing their feelings and needs, either emotionally or verbally. In fact, they are often almost oblivious to all feelings except happiness and anger. Sadness, hurt, disappointment, regret, feelings of inadequacy and vulnerability, are all channeled into and expressed in one emotion: explosive anger.

A final characteristic of violent men is their total emotional dependence on the women they batter. Apart from that relationship their lives are emotional voids. Battering is an attack on this deficiency in themselves, which is projected on to the woman. Their dependency is often expressed in exaggerated jealousy. The abusing husband will accumulate real or imagined evidence that his wife is involved in some relationship outside the marriage, which often causes him to eliminate all of his wife's contacts outside the home. Thus she becomes tied to him in an unhealthy way. Unfortunately, many women who come to shelters feel a strong need to go back to the abusive home because they know that their husbands are so emotionally dependent on them.

A cycle of violence is a frequent pattern engaged in by abusive people. This pattern may be repeated every few days, once a week, once a month, or over a period of several months. As tension builds during the first phase, the wife walks on egg shells, hoping she will do nothing to set off the violence. However, it is not her behavior but the emotional condition of the man himself that triggers it. After the violence stops, the husband will go through a time of repentance and will promise that his behavior will never happen again. And then the cycle starts all over again. Note the following diagram:

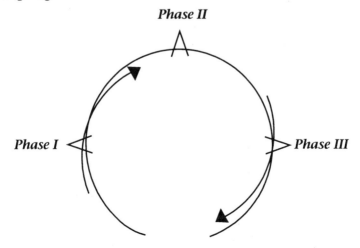

Phase I *Tension Builds*	**Phase II** *Explosion*	**Phase III** *Honeymoon*
• stress • minor incidents of battering • woman tries to cope; stays out of man's way • woman tries to avoid violence by "correct" behavior • woman denies future in order to cope	• acute battering incident • lack of predictability • lack of control • phase may last 24 hours to 1 week • woman may call police, flee to shelter, etc. • shock and denial	• man is loving, kind, contrite, apologetic • denial of violence • man promises to change

What Can Be Done?

As a society we face the enormous task of reevaluating as well as working to change the family structures and cultural conditions that have produced violent men. We need to teach men the meaning of love and of true personhood and how to express emotions. Males need to address their drive to dominate and control. Homes need to become places where children are disciplined in love and taught how to serve others, places where adults and children work together to build up one another's self-esteem.

As Christians we need to abandon the platonic dualism mentioned above and return to the scriptural teachings that the image of God is present in both males and females. We also need to reexamine what the New Testament teaches (Eph. 5) about mutual submission and love between husband and wife. Nowhere in the Bible is a husband given the responsibility to rule over or discipline—certainly not to use physical force with—his wife (for more information see *Agenda for Synod 1992*, pp. 328-333, Christian Reformed Church in North America).

Our understanding of suffering for righteousness sake also needs reexamination. The suffering of battered women is imposed against their will and accomplishes only harm. It is inflicted because of someone else's neglect and cruelty. The suffering the Bible teaches us to bear is accepted voluntarily in obedience to Christ's calling. It accomplishes good for God's kingdom and benefits the sufferer. Thus the apostle Paul chose to suffer for the gospel out of love for the Lord and to lead others to Christ. His suffering had a purpose and was blessed. The suffering of abuse has no purpose and can never be blessed.

What We Can and Should Do

First, it is important to make very clear that the violence must stop. Call it what it is: a cruel sin against a being created in the image of God and behavior for which God requires genuine repentance. We must reject any rationalization or blaming of the victim. No matter what the circumstances, violence is never permissible.

Second, we should offer hope for change. Group treatment programs designed for batterers seem to be the most effective. As a Christian community we must work in conjunction with secular programs to bring about change in violent men; we lack the education and resources to do that alone.

Third, we must hold the batterer accountable. Many promises to change are made during the honeymoon phase of the cycle of violence, but few men go for treatment. If a man is really serious about changing, he must enter and stick to a treatment program. A batterer is like an alcoholic—he needs to battle the impulse for the rest of his life.

As much as we loathe, as a Christian community, causing couples to separate, it is often important to remove the batterer from the home or to place the battered person in a protective shelter. Marital therapy will not work unless the violence has stopped and the husband is in a treatment program. Premature marital counseling may actually endanger the victim further.

The following are specific things we can do for a battered wife. First, we must believe the story the woman tells and not challenge it or make excuses for her husband. We must recognize that she is only telling us a small part of what is really going on in the home.

Second, as we listen, we should remember that her self-esteem has been greatly damaged by the abuse. She is dealing with feelings of guilt and despair, struggling with moral questions related to leaving her husband. We should assure her of confidentiality, assist her in getting medical care, and promise to help her to find a shelter for battered women.

Third, we must not suggest marital counseling as a way to heal her marriage; that only prolongs the abuse. We should tell her that she needs protection and her husband needs to get into a treatment program.

There are three basic goals to keep in mind when dealing with battered women.

1. Protect the victim from further abuse and act as her advocate in society.
2. Stop the abuse through some legal means or through the confrontation of an authority figure her husband respects.
3. Restore the relationship or mourn its loss. Recognize that violence can so destroy a relationship that it is past saving. A single-parent home where wife and children are safe is sociologically, psychologically, and theologically better than a two-parent home in which violence occurs.

Child Physical and Sexual Abuse

Where there is violence against the wife, there may also be physical and sexual abuse of the children. In homes where domestic violence occurs, children are physically abused or seriously neglected at a rate 1,500 percent higher than in the general population.

Even when the children are not physically abused, witnessing domestic violence (true for an estimated three million children per year) has emotional effects very similar to the trauma of being a victim of child abuse. These effects include taking responsibility for the abuse, constant anxiety that another battering will occur, guilt for not being able to stop the abuse or for loving the abuser, and fear of being abandoned.

Children in violent homes may experience cognitive or language problems, developmental delays, and stress-related physical problems, such as headaches, ulcers, and hearing and speech difficulties. Boys who witness their mothers being beaten are more likely to become batterers. No evidence exists, however, that girls in similar situations have a higher risk of being battered themselves as adults.

Each year in the United States an estimated two million children are physically abused. Included in this statistic are reports of any physical injuries inflicted on a child by an adult perpetrated out of anger or a desire to control, dominate, or intimidate. Not included are cases of verbal and emotional abuse, which are almost impossible to quantify. (For a brief critique of a Christian attempt to justify such physical abuse, see Appendix C, "The Rod of Discipline.")

Even more insidious and grotesque than physical abuse is the prevalent sexual abuse, which is defined as follows:

> Child sexual abuse is any forced sexual contact upon a child who developmentally is not capable of understanding or resisting, and/or who is socially or emotionally dependent upon the offender. Abuse may include fondling, masturbation, genital penetration, or exhibitionism. It is a crime in every state (Carlson 1998, 11).

One in four female and one in seven male children will be sexually assaulted beginning at preadolescence—an average of eight years of age. It is four times more likely that this sexual molestation will occur inside rather than outside the home. Fathers and stepfathers of the victims make up almost half of all sexual offenders. Often the victims grow up to become sexual abusers themselves, thus perpetuating a destructive cycle generation after generation.

Sexual abuse of children has been going on for a long time, but awareness of it has been suffocated by silence and disbelief. In the late 1890s Sigmund Freud began to study "female hysteria." After many interviews he concluded that the origin of every case of hysteria was childhood sexual trauma caused by fathers.

However, Freud was not comfortable with this discovery because of what it said about men who were considered socially respectable. Accordingly, he falsified the data and stated that sexual trauma was caused by governesses, nurses, maids, and other children of both sexes. Later Freud publicly denounced his findings and said that they must have been the fantasies of women. But in private letters he acknowledged widespread sexual abuse by fathers. He also expressed anxiety about his desires towards his own daughters and suspicions about his own father.

As recently as 1975 a basic American psychiatry textbook estimated the frequency of all forms of incest as only one in a million.

In the legal profession there has been widespread prejudice against child victims, particularly in the past. The most famous legal text published in this country, John Henry Wigmores' *Treatise on Evidence* (1934), impeaches the credibility of any female, especially a child, who complains of a sex offense. The McMartin School case, the most expensive and lengthy trial in the history of the United States, is a good example of how adults question the credibility of children. The McMartin jury did not believe the children's allegations of sexual abuse. Rather, they believed that the children had been asked leading questions and that it was impossible to distinguish their fanciful stories from possible truth. Since the law requires that defendants be found guilty beyond a reasonable doubt, the school staff was acquitted. Most modern research indicates, however, that children lie about sexual abuse in only a very few cases.

In a paper entitled "In Thy Father's House: Incest in Conservative Christian Homes," Dr. Vincent E. Gil reported that incest is prevalent in the conservative Christian community as well. In the cases analyzed in his report, fifty-eight percent of the girls were abused by their fathers and forty-two percent by their stepfathers.

Even if they don't report the molestation, children who are being abused will often exhibit sexually inappropriate behavior, for example, grabbing the genitals of others, dressing in sexually provocative clothes, or using sexually explicit language.

A common feeling that victims have is fear. They are afraid of what their fathers or stepfathers are going to do to them next. Thy have an even greater fear that no one would believe them if they reported what happened.

In almost all cases of incest the children feel some responsibility for the abuse, believing that they must have said or done the wrong thing or dressed in the wrong way. This feeling often leads to a cycle of guilt, which destroys what is left of their self-esteem and leads to acceptance of more abuse.

Often the abusers feel the same way as their victims. They are afraid of being found out. They may also feel hidden guilt about what they are doing, guilt that leads to lower self-esteem and, in turn, to more abuse.

Most abusers also develop emotional defenses about their acts, such as denying the abuse or projecting onto others responsibility for it. These defenses are commonly used when they face other problems in their lives. Their sexual attraction toward children may have developed at an early age, and/or they may be unable to relate sexually with adults.

An emotional need to control is often at the heart of a molester's problem. As is true of spousal batterers, most offenders are the "kings of their castles," and the abuse is an expression of their absolute authority. They completely dominate their wives and their children. Many such men are also substance abusers.

Often the victim of abuse is the oldest or only daughter, the responsible child and the little mother of the family. Since she typically takes on many of the mother's tasks, the father regards her as the one who must carry out the wife's sexual responsibilities. In a sexually abusive family the mother is usually an emotionally weak woman, controlled by a very dominant husband.

Sometimes the mother is unaware of the problem; the daughter, however, usually believes that the mother does know but doesn't try to stop it, which causes alienation between daughter and mother. There are situations in which the mother has had an extended illness, so the father pursues one of his daughters; the daughter may believe, however, that she is being offered by her mother as a substitute.

In one study of female victims the girls displayed strong animosity towards their mothers but had fond memories of their fathers, perhaps because incest victims often receive special presents and treatment from their abusers. The girls were more tolerant of the shortcomings of their fathers than the failures of their mothers.

When the truth eventually does surface, daughters are often disappointed at their mothers' responses. Some mothers refuse to believe their daughters and defend the abuser. Even if the mother does believe her child and forces the father to leave home, often that situation only lasts for short time.

Other mothers are more sympathetic to the plight of their daughters. When the horror, which they might have suspected, is revealed, they express shock. They often feel guilt, embarrassment, and intense anger toward their husband, forcing him to leave the home.

As in the case of battered women the ultimate goal is to restore all family relationships. However, depending on the intensity of the abuse and the complexity of the problems, this cannot always be accomplished. It is important, as with spousal abuse, that sudden explosions of repentance on the part of the abuser be viewed with extreme skepticism unless he has been in a treatment program for some time.

Steps We Can and Should Take

Our response to abuse should always be to seek justice. We should express righteous anger and compassion for the victim; the child must be believed and supported emotionally. We should be advocates for the victim; abused children are frequently powerless to seek justice against their abusers. We should hold the offender accountable for his actions and require an admission of guilt, repentance, and restitution. And we should work towards prevention; now that the abuse is known, we must make sure it will not continue.

It is important to deal with all the long-term emotional needs of the victim. In cases of father-daughter incest the first relationship that needs to be restored is the one between mother and daughter. The guilt and self-blame of the victim should be dealt with as well as the inevitable confusion, fear about the future, and anger. Victims need ways to build up their self-esteem and assertiveness, and they need to gain new understanding in all areas of human sexuality. This is best done through skilled counselors working in private or group support counseling. Pastors and concerned friends can also be a means of support and encouragement.

Care for the mother is much like that for the daughter because emotional needs are similar. The mother must admit her complicity, ignorance, or denial, and together with the daughter share anger, outrage, and feelings of betrayal. Perhaps through private and group therapy mother and daughter will be able to trust each other again. The wife also has to deal with her future relationship with her husband, as well as with a lack of self-esteem and feelings of inadequacy.

Care for the offender is more complex and controversial. Many agree that, after the abuse has been discovered, the abuser should be asked to leave the home. If the child is forced to leave that only adds to her feelings of unworthiness. In situations of father-daughter incest the father's absence will often help to facilitate renewed mother-daughter bonding.

Two types of programs are advocated for offenders; one recommends therapy alone and the other, therapy combined with imprisonment. Actual imprisonment, or the threat of it, may help to keep batterers and child sexual offenders in treatment.

Programs for sexual offenders are structured much like those for substance abusers. This is necessary because many offenders abuse substances as well and because sexual abuse is an addiction. The abuser needs to deal with the issue of control and who or what controls his life. Once he is able to give up control to a higher power, there is hope that he will be able to live a respectable life.

Unfortunately, the complex and sinful problems of domestic violence and child abuse are also present within the church. We need to break the existing code of silence and reexamine some of the theological views that have supported and perpetuated these abominations before God.

FOR PERSONAL PREPARATION

Recall whether the subject of battered women has come up for discussion in your church at any time. Or do you remember as a child hearing family talk about some neighbor woman, family friend, or church member who had been battered? How did your parent comment on this? If it was a church member, how did your church respond? How did you feel about the matter then? How do you feel now?

Were you ever spanked as a child? Did you think that was cruel of your parents? How did you respond to that spanking? Have you ever spanked your own children? Did you do it in anger? If so, how did you feel after the anger subsided?

Chapter Eight

THE CRISIS OF DIVORCE

Labeled the "Never Ending Crisis" by Norman Wright, divorce is often never completely resolved. For those involved many events continually remind them of the brokenness of their lives.

A family funeral may be such an event. Some years ago I conducted the funeral of a man who had been divorced from his wife for sixteen years. Bitterness and cruelty were a part of the marriage's breakup. The only son had sided with his mother and gone to live with her, while the only daughter had sided and lived with her father. Before the father's death the son had been reconciled with him, but the estranged wife had never visited the hospital. At the funeral, however, the ex-wife sat in the front row with her children and received the attention due a grieving widow. That caused great stress and emotional pain for the daughter. After the funeral the family war continued with renewed intensity.

A family wedding may also salt the wounds of a divorce. Weddings remind everyone of the tragedy of broken vows. The bride may be torn between whether her father or stepfather should walk her down the aisle. People may wonder—how should everyone involved be listed in the program? Where should certain people sit during the ceremony? These and many similar questions heighten the stress of the wedding ceremony for the young couple. We listen to the couple recite their vows before God and those present, and we pray that God will give them a happy life until death separates them. At the same time we recognize that the brokenness of marital bonds has left an indelible impression on them and given them an example that, as statistics indicate, will be hard for them to avoid duplicating.

The divorce rate in the United States has risen steadily over the past one hundred years from two divorces for every 1,000 marriages in 1879 to twenty-two per 1,000 in 1979. In the 1980s the rate leveled off to around twenty divorces for every 1,000 marriages, a rate that is higher than in any other country and in any other time in history.

By most estimates one out of every three current marriages will end in the divorce courts. The average length of marriages that end in divorce is seven years, and the rate of divorce is highest in marriages of two to three years duration. Divorce is more likely to occur when there is a sizable age gap between the couple or there are differences in religion, social class, or ethnic origin.

Divorce in the Church

For many years the church considered divorce a problem for the world, not for Christians. But today divorce is very much a part of the church's life, with Protestants having a higher rate than Catholics or Jews.

In the past most conservative churches handled divorce by shunning or removing the offending parties; divorced persons were shoved out of sight so that others weren't tempted to follow their bad example. Churches also looked for easy formulas to determine who was at fault. If adultery was discovered, that made divorce more acceptable. But if adultery was not an issue, the one who filed for divorce was identified as the guilty party, or perhaps the one who had moved out, or the one who had stopped attending church.

Some of these ideas persist in the church today, but they only serve to make the crisis of divorce greater. At times formal discipline by the church is useful and necessary, but it must never be based on some easy formula. Rather, the Christian community should strive for a better understanding of this crisis as well as of the biblical teaching regarding it and proceed with wisdom in ministering to those involved.

What Does the Bible Say?

The Pharisees tested Jesus on the subject of marriage and divorce (Matt. 5:31-32; 19:3-9; Mark 10:2-12). They asked the following question: What does God consider an acceptable reason for divorce? (Luke 16:18). But Jesus told them that they were looking at the issue from the wrong viewpoint and refused to directly answer the question.

Instead, Jesus reminded them that in the beginning God created male and female for the purpose of bringing them together in a lifelong union of oneness. He said that what God brings together we are not to break apart, that in marriage a triangular relationship is formed between the Lord, the husband, and the wife; this new relationship reflects the oneness of the trinity.

We, however, do not live in the perfect world that God created. Our world is full of sin and broken relationships. God calls us to reflect his ideal through the grace of the Lord Jesus, but not all marriages, even among Christians, are able to reach or maintain that ideal. Like Moses in the Old Testament, Jesus reminds us that divorce is the result of hard hearts, first hardened toward God and then toward others.

When Jesus spoke about divorce because of adultery, he was not giving a ground for divorce but only an example of how the hardening process can destroy the bonds of marriage. There are no grounds for divorce, not even adultery. The offended spouse should be gently counseled to work through the process of forgiveness. But in certain situations the adulterer will not respond to calls of repentance and reconciliation, and the relationship is broken beyond repair.

In the final analysis the reason for the failure of any marriage is sin. God hates divorce today as much as he did in Malachi's day (Mal. 2:10-16). Created by God, marriage is a divine institution in which a man and a woman enjoy each other's uniqueness and serve the Lord together. Christ calls all couples to fidelity in marriage as a lifelong commitment. This call, however, does not reflect a greater commitment to the institution than it does to the individual people involved. Marriage was made for humankind, not humankind for marriage.

Emphasizing the institution over the person was a constant source of contention between Jesus and the Pharisees. To the Pharisees, maintaining an institution was more important than the spiritual welfare of the people—their tedious rules about the observance of the Sabbath Day provide an example of this trait. Jesus constantly told them that the Sabbath was made for man, not man for the Sabbath.

The Pharisees wanted to produce a specific spiritual product through rules and regulations. But Jesus came to reconcile us to God through grace and forgiveness. When the Jews wanted Jesus to condemn the woman caught in adultery, he called all the people, including the woman, to examine themselves and leave their lives of sin. When Jesus spoke to the Samaritan woman, he did not condemn her because of her five broken marriages but instead offered redemption and a new start.

To be sure, divorce should not be treated lightly, but it should be treated redemptively. No one should seek a divorce except in situations where exhaustive pastoral and therapeutic efforts have failed to end an adulterous relationship or an abusive situation continues to exist. Divorce should not be sought just because of "irreconcilable differences." There are, however, certain sad times when one spouse has to acquiesce in the decision of the other to seek a divorce.

Simply a legal procedure, divorce itself is not a sin. The sin lies in the events that destroyed the marriage relationship, in the disregard for the vows taken before God, in the putting asunder of what God has joined together. It is the sin, not the legal procedure, that should move the body of Christ into restoring those who are going astray.

Although it is certainly regrettable, the destruction of a marriage relationship is not an unpardonable sin. When those who have sinned express genuine sorrow and seek forgiveness, they must be received and restored as members of the body of Christ. Each week when we worship, the word of God calls us to repentance, forgiveness, and a new start. This applies to every area of our lives. The Christian message promises that out of brokenness can come forgiveness and restoration. As we minister to those going through the crisis of divorce, we offer this message, which is available to everyone.

The Six Stages of Divorce

Ministry to those going through the crisis of divorce will be most beneficial when we understand the many dimensions of the divorce process. Counselors have pointed out the following stages of a divorce:

Stage 1: Emotional Divorce

This stage begins when one or both of the spouses begin to withhold emotional support from the other. Feelings become concentrated on the negative rather than the positive areas of the spouse's personality. And a person begins to recognize that he is no longer "number one" to his spouse.

"Disillusionment" and "detachment" are the best words to portray the marriage relationship at this point. Someone has described it as a process of dying a series of emotional deaths. At the beginning of the marriage there was a long sequence of emotional investments, but at this stage one spouse or perhaps both are directing their emotional energy toward searching out new things and new people in which to invest emotionally. During this time spouses fantasize about relationships that could have been or might possibly be. They begin to imagine life without the other person.

Unfortunately, a couple may be caught in this stage throughout the marriage. Though never separated or divorced, they remain in a state of emotional detachment from each other and fail to improve their relationship.

Marriage is much more than a wedding ceremony; it is a process of becoming one, a process that must never stop in our imperfect world. With the words "What God has joined together, let not man put asunder" the Bible calls all couples to a lifelong commitment to become one in Jesus Christ. When couples fail to continue this joining process, they are tearing apart what God has joined together.

Married people should analyze their own marriages before judging those who are going through the crisis of divorce. One couple may be saying publicly that they are no longer emotionally attached, while many others may be hiding that same truth behind self-righteous condemnations of divorce. God sees the hypocrisy in our hearts. The Bible tells us not to look at the speck in another's eye while neglecting the beam in our own (Matt. 7:3). Instead, one couple's public crisis should cause all couples to reevaluate their own marital relationship before the Lord.

Stage 2: Legal Divorce

At this stage one or both of the spouses may retain a lawyer and go through the legal process of dividing up the property and deciding on custody of any children. In many states laws have been changed to make dissolution of a marriage a relatively simple procedure, but for most people this does not make divorce any less of a crisis. Although the legal process provides dissolution of the marriage, it does not provide release from the emotional pain.

During the legal phase a decision has to be made about which spouse will leave the home, a decision that can cause great stress for every family member. Such a separation is disruptive for all involved; it requires a massive family reorganization of rules, roles, standards, and boundaries.

It is important that the couple receive emotional support from family, friends, and church members during this time. But we must be cautious in our support. Each spouse may perceive such support as proof that he or she is in the right and use it as a weapon against the other. Support given by the Christian community should be neutral and objective. It should involve listening and sharing in the stress and grief of the entire family.

Stage 3: Economic Divorce

The third stage usually alters a person's lifestyle. Often the woman is forced to get a job to support her family; ninety-eight percent of all single-parent households are headed by women. Studies show that two-thirds of single-parent families live below the poverty level. There is also evidence that new laws, such as no-fault divorce in California, have had disastrous effects. One study concluded that in the ten years since this law was instituted, divorced women and their children suffered a seventy-three percent drop in their standard of living while ex-husbands experienced a forty-two percent increase during the first year.

Some couples are able to agree on a division of the property and financial responsibilities, but for others resentments, hostilities, and feelings of revenge prevent equitable solutions. Decisions about spousal and child support often provide the biggest problems. I know of one divorced couple who, after nine years of separation, are still fighting over child support payments. Many fathers are delinquent in such support; often this is another way for them to get back at their ex-wives.

In California child-support matters are becoming less combative and litigious. The computer age has made life a little simpler for mothers seeking proper support. All the pertinent financial records for both wife and husband are entered into a computer, and the program determines the amount of monthly support.

During the struggles over finances, concerned Christians should stand for justice. Combative spouses should be counseled to understand that money is not the real issue. Anger and desire for revenge or control only hurt themselves and any children involved.

Stage 4: Co-Parental Divorce

Spouses are divorced from each other but not from their children, although many children caught in this situation feel as if this is the case. Parents should be encouraged to work cooperatively on problems of custody, visitation, and finances. It is a time to mourn the loss of the intact family and to restructure the parent-child relationships to fit the reality that some family members will be living apart.

The divorce process can be as easy or as hard on children as the parents wish to make it. If the spouses allow themselves to be controlled by anger and bitterness, if they try to justify themselves by placing all the blame on the other, they can force the children to take sides. That is a serious mistake and a form of emotional abuse of their children.

Stage 5: Community Divorce

This stage is characterized by loneliness, caused by a change in social status. While married, the couple socialized with other couples. Now, feeling like the proverbial "fifth wheel," they may no longer fit into this couples' world.

A divorced person may have been a leader in some area of the church's life. Church members may now wonder what is best for the group as well as for the individual. Do we force the person to resign or encourage her to continue on in that position? This is not an easy decision because asking the person to resign may mean putting her through another loss, which will increase feelings of guilt and isolation.

Often church members don't know what to say to a person going through the crisis of divorce. Our reactions often reflect our own insecurities. We should be aware of the common reactions that everyone, even family and close friends, typically have toward a person in this predicament.

The first reaction is often anxiety. Perhaps family and friends viewed the marriage as a healthy one, even as a model to others. Now they may fear that if this seemingly healthy marriage could fall apart, their own could as well.

Another reaction may be shame. This is especially true if family and friends are experiencing similar problems and know they are not taking any steps to improve their own marriages.

Some react by becoming preoccupied with the divorce, always talking about it, and wanting to know more and more about the relationship. While it's good to show concern for the person going through the divorce, too many personal questions show little tact and a lack of genuine empathy.

Even in the Christian community people may have fantasies about a sexual relationship with one of the partners. A divorced woman may suddenly receive an inordinate amount of attention from male friends, attention under the guise of wanting to help her get through a difficult time. Unfortunately, many men believe in the "divorced woman syndrome," a myth perpetuating the idea that divorced women have enhanced sexual interest. In fact, most divorced women report a severe decrease in sexual desire because of the loss of self-worth they experience at this time.

Strange as it may seem, some people gain pleasure from the suffering and failure of others. If the divorced couple were prominent, wealthy, had social status, or an abundance of talent, envious people may view with pleasure the failure of their marital relationship.

Another reaction to those who are divorcing may be a feeling of superiority. Some people may look down upon divorced people as either weak and inferior or quitters and sinners. This reaction is often found in long-married couples who wonder what has gone wrong with the younger generation.

Sad to say, such feelings of superiority are even found within the church community. At times church members treat divorced people like lepers were treated in Jesus' day. They think a divorced person should have no public visibility in the church but should "fade into the woodwork." They treat divorce as a contagious disease and fear others who associate with such people will catch the divorce "bug."

Shock and denial are another common reaction—"It can't be!" "Go to a counselor!" "Think about the children!" If the conflict between the marriage partners has been particularly intense, friends may feel the frustration of thinking they have to take sides. Depression is also not uncommon among those whose friends are experiencing this crisis.

To have a beneficial ministry to those in the throes of a divorce, we need to understand our own reactions to and feelings about divorce as well as the insecurities we may have about our own marriage relationships.

Stage 6: Psychic Divorce

During this final stage the divorced person seeks to become autonomous by emotionally separating from the influence and presence of the former spouse. This is the most difficult stage. It can, however, be a time in which the person learns to become whole again, a time of reflection on his relationship to God and his own responsibilities. It can also be a time to begin making good changes. This stage is especially important if one ever hopes to marry again. If these tasks are never completed, the negative relational patterns of the previous marriage will contribute to failures in the next one.

Coping with Divorce

The transitional period of a divorce is a process that may take two years or more. As a person proceeds through the six stages mentioned above, they also experience an underlying grief process. Divorce causes many "deaths" in one's life, losses that must be acknowledged and grieved.

There is the loss of the marriage relationship, of growing old together, planning family vacations, burning the mortgage, and settling into a retirement community. There is the loss of the intact family unit as well as the loss of love, contentment, comfort, security, and many hopes and dreams. Besides the tangible and present losses, there are many abstract and future ones, significant nonetheless.

In ministering to a person who is going through a divorce, it is important for all to remember that the couple is experiencing an intense grieving process, one that can, at times, be more acute than grief over a loved one's physical death. If a person dies, the spouse can grieve the loss and go on. But in a divorce, the spouse does not die; he may live in the same city, the same neighborhood. She may have to have frequent interaction with him because of the children. Thus the pain may go on and on.

The rejected spouse may hope that her marriage may be reconstituted. I talked with a divorce woman who didn't want to take her ex-husband to court over child support. The reasons she gave seemed quite noble, but when we cut away all the dross, the real reason was that as long as the matter was unsettled she had an excuse to be involved in his life and could hope that some day they might remarry.

After the initial shock a divorced person will experience the normal stages of grief, depression, anger, guilt, ambivalence toward life, loss of energy, and finally acceptance and a desire to make new attachments. Just as in the case of a physical death, it is very important for people caught in this crisis to complete the task of grieving before pursuing another relationship. If another marriage is entered into prematurely, the uncompleted tasks of grieving will cause destructive relational patterns to develop in that marriage as well.

How people going through a divorce actually cope with this crisis will depend upon a number of factors—the first to be considered is whether they have an adequate perception of the situation. Divorce is a great loss. Along with the obvious losses will come a loss of identity and role mastery as well as of nurturance. It is important for a person in this situation to make sense of the situation and his role in it.

A second important coping factor is an adequate social network. In the past the church has often abandoned those going through a divorce, especially those perceived to be the guilty parties. If we are going to work redemptively with each other, however, we must not withdraw from these people but rather provide the support they need. It is often said that we should not condone what they have done, but by pulling away we only make the crisis worse and create additional hurts that may never be healed.

If a person is going to deal constructively with this crisis, he must also have adequate coping mechanisms. Bible reading and prayer are most important at this time. Many good books are also available to help in making practical decisions. And members of support groups can share wisdom gained from their experience.

Children and Divorce

The generally held belief that children adjust adequately to most divorce situations has been proven false. In her book *Second Chances: Men, Women, and Children a Decade after Divorce,* Judith Wallerstein points out that divorced families suffer much psychological damage.

Children of divorce suffer from underachievement, anger, worry, low self-esteem, feelings of abandonment, and inability to set goals. Other studies have shown that such children have a higher high school dropout rate, inferior communication skills, and poorer overall physical health than children from intact families. On an even more troubling note, children of divorce have a higher rate of adolescent sexual activity and drug use. Keeping these disturbing facts in mind, we must remember that an estimated half of all children born today will live in a single-parent home some time before they reach the age of eighteen.

As Christians we should be very concerned about the special effect divorce has on children who have been raised in Christian homes. Divorce inevitably shakes their faith to the core. All their lives they have been taught about love, forgiveness, and trust. Life at home modeled their understanding of God. Divorce leaves them with many questions about God's faithfulness and love. Those contemplating divorce should be reminded of what Jesus said about anyone who would cause one of these little ones to stumble (Matt. 18:6).

David Bredehoft, in his article "Predictable Passages Through Divorce," develops a model to help us understand the different stages children go through during the process of divorce. These children are also experiencing a grieving process, so all the predictable aspects of grieving will be present in the various stages.

Fear is a child's initial response to the trauma of divorce. Predictable in young children, it has also been observed in adolescents and older children. At first the child feels an overwhelming concern about his personal welfare, often worrying about being forgotten or abandoned by both parents. Some younger

| *The Scare* |
| *The Cause* |
| *The Cure* |
| *The Power* |
| *The Dream* |
| *The Acceptance* |

children will wander around aimlessly crying; such children need assurance that they will be cared for and their needs met. During this "scare" time many children make insatiable demands for attention. They are attempting to make sense out of their chaotic world and need a constant empathetic support system.

Children will often give accurate information about their problems but lack the experience to interpret those problems. Typically, they see their parents' behavior as a response to something they themselves have done. Consequently, they often conclude that they have caused the divorce. It is important that parents explain the reasons for the divorce honestly and assure the children that they are not to blame.

Many children of divorce think that they can somehow solve the problem; they will engage in a process that is similar to bargaining during the dying process. To be sure, there are similarities—their family is dying, and the children want to do anything they can to prevent that death. Some will plan and ingeniously stage a crisis so that both parents have to come together again, hoping this will restore the family. Parents and concerned friends should be aware of the children's attempts to repair the marriage and make clear that whatever the children may do, the decision made by the parents is final.

Throughout the entire divorce process parents are vulnerable to manipulation. Much of their time and effort is consumed in dealing with their own problems and emotional pain. Children understand this quickly and thereby gain considerable power. Frequently they will use this power to manipulate a situation that forces the parents back together or plays off one parent against the other in order to accomplish what is on their agenda.

Many children feel anger and resentment toward one or both parents for breaking up the family. Often these feelings are acted out in the form of power. Some mothers report having to ask their children if they can go out on a date. It is not uncommon for sons to exercise this power by assuming the tasks that their fathers previously did. But when a child's power does not achieve the desired goal, a sense of powerlessness and depression often results.

Children of divorce create fantasies about the reunion of their parents. Even children who have been abused by one or both of their parents dream about the time when they will be reunited as a family. Divorced children cling tightly to the dream to help them cope with the reality that their family has broken apart and their parents no longer love each other. The dream provides a ray of hope, which the children use to make their past congruent with their future.

Children do not come to a total acceptance of divorce until they give up this dream of reconciling their parents. True acceptance comes when a child faces the reality of the situation. If a child was quite young when the divorce occurred, this process may take several years. Parents, relatives, and friends should not retard this adjustment by feeding the child's dream and assuring him that someday a reconciliation of the parents will occur.

Some responses of children to separation and divorce are unique to their age and developmental skills. Preschoolers-to-early-elementary children will display the most fear. Because they can't understand what is going on, the situation feels very "scary." This age group will use "magical thinking," in which they see themselves as masters of their universe. They will often display short-term regression to babyish behavior in an attempt to insure parental care.

Early-to-mid-elementary children can understand what death, dying, and divorce mean. They will often respond with intense sadness, which breaks down their ability to cope with the crisis. Many have fantasies of being deprived of food, toys, or some other important part of their usual routine, fantasies that may result in compulsive overeating, begging, or wheedling gifts.

A fully conscious, intense anger is most typical of older-elementary-to-early-adolescent children. Their anger is usually clearly directed, well-organized, and articulate. Older children view the world in absolutes, as black and white. They have little ability to deal with subtleties and ambiguities.

At this age, because they have learned to be unswervingly loyal to friends and team members, children are particularly vulnerable to siding with one parent against the other. And because their identity is so closely tied to the external family structure, these youngsters often experience confusion and a threat of ruptured identity when parents separate. Feelings of shame may lead them to attempt to conceal the divorce, and their emotions about it, from the outside world.

Adolescents view divorce as a situation in which their parents choose to leave them before they have the chance to gradually separate from their families. They worry about whether their family relationships will remain alive or die with the dying marriage. Divorce threatens to destroy the concept of family as a safe base to which teens can return to replenish depleted emotional supplies. They feel they have lost the place to which they could return to restore battered self-esteem, to regress briefly, to retreat temporarily, and to gather courage for the next venture into independence.

An acute sense of loneliness, fear, and confusion can develop when the teen finds her parents unavailable because they are preoccupied with their own needs and unable to give much energy to the adolescent's problems. Anger is also a common response. It masks feelings of vulnerability and powerlessness. It helps shut out pain and expresses resentment at one or both of the parents for presuming to give their own wishes priority over the needs of their children.

Divorce brings extraordinary losses. We should never seek a God-allowed reason to excuse divorce, like the Pharisees did, but rather work as hard as possible to avoid it. Still, this should not exempt us from providing the best possible redemptive ministry to those who are suffering its inevitable pain. More than ever they need the healing power of the Savior in their lives.

FOR PERSONAL PREPARATION

Ask yourself whether your church deals with divorce now the same way that it did twenty-five or more years ago. What changes have taken place? Do you approve or disapprove of those changes? Are there other changes that you think should be made?

Consider also how you and others in the church respond to families who are going through the crisis of divorce. Do you tend to distance yourselves from such a family as if it has some sort of infectious disease? Do you tend to take sides, giving support to one of the parties? What do you do to recognize and carry something of the pain that these people are experiencing?

Appendix A

WHAT ABOUT ANGER?

Many Christians struggle with feelings of anger in the dying and grieving process. They believe that Christians should never get angry, that their anger is a sin or a lack of faith. Because anger produces guilt, it is often never properly dealt with and can lead to further emotional problems. However, anger can be seen as a God-given source of creative energy, which helps us move beyond obstacles. These obstacles would normally block or discourage us because of our depleted resources.

Powerful though it may be, anger is a secondary emotion. Other feelings cause us to become angry—fear, lack of control, hurt, loss. Whenever we become angry, we need to try to discover what other emotion is really the cause.

Anger affects us in a variety of ways. Physiologically, it speeds up our pulse, constricts our blood vessels, and increases our adrenaline. Intellectually, it turns us toward the past (such as past debts owed us), makes our mind race, and focuses us so intensely on whatever is blocking us that we become blind to other possibilities. Emotionally, anger upsets our normal equilibrium and turns our attention to hurts—real or imagined, physical or emotional.

Anger also affects our behavior. We fear this emotion because it can evoke action that is socially unacceptable. Everyday annoyance and frustration may become resentment, aggression, and rage. These emotions often find no adequate or meaningful outlet or resolution. Consequently, most of us don't deal effectively with anger.

From youth to adulthood we learn to fear anger. When adults became angry, they hit us or yelled at us. Thus we concluded that anger must be wrong. This feeling that anger was associated with punishment may have been reinforced by a Christian association of anger with sin. Remember what happened to Moses when he got angry and struck the rock (Num. 20:2-15)? We may have been told that it makes Jesus sad to see us angry.

But does the Bible really teach that it is a sin to get angry? It does warn us against the effects of anger (Matt. 5:21, 22; Prov. 22:24, 25; 29:22). It tells us anger is a dangerous emotion if it is misused, harmful to others, and destructive to ourselves. Yet the Psalmist does not deny anger but says, "Be angry and sin not" (Ps. 4:4). And David expressed his anger in Psalm 109: 5-14; we all have probably spoken that angry prayer at some time in our lives.

The most common Hebrew word for anger is "aph," a word with the root meaning of blowing or snorting through nostrils. The Bible says that God "aphed" the spirit that gave human life. Accordingly, anger and spirit are closely connected in the Bible. Spirit is expressive of the healthy side of anger. When someone has spirit, we usually think of that person as being lively, as someone who expresses the full range of emotions, including anger. Spirited persons are animated, the opposite of depressed. It is important to note that most depression is caused by repressed anger.

In the Old Testament the Hebrew word for anger is used 177 times in relation to God and forty-five times in relation to humans. If God experiences anger, it can hardly be a sin for us to experience the same emotion. Thus anger is neither right nor wrong.

How we deal with the emotion of anger is the key. Paul said, "Be angry, and sin not. Do not let the sun go down on your anger" (Eph. 4:26). We need to consider how anger affects us and develop a proper response.

As indicated earlier, anger affects us emotionally, therefore we need to decipher the emotion that caused the anger. Another person's actions may have helped us to become angry, but the person didn't actually make us angry. That is a choice we made. The first step in responding properly is to ask, "Why am I angry? Why did I choose to react in this way?"

Anger affects us physically as well. There are, however, ways we can release the pressure in our bodies caused by our anger. Exercise is a good release of tension. Relaxation techniques can also be helpful.

And anger affects us intellectually. We decide to be angry. Unfortunately, we are not always aware of making a conscious choice. Instead of being obsessed with past hurts and grievances, we should look to the future and ask, "Where do I go from here?"

Obviously, anger affects our behavior. We may choose to strike out verbally or physically—a very common response. Some even suggest this is the best way to rid ourselves of anger. Another common reaction is passive-aggressive behavior, in which a person doesn't express anger directly. He may revert to more subtle yet destructive responses, such as tardiness, avoidance, blaming, or complaining. Crude or cutting remarks are often expressions of passive-aggressive behavior.

It is always important to clarify the "why" of the anger. What other feeling has actually brought this emotion to the forefront? Perhaps the anger could be the result of something that happened earlier in the day or at another time. For example, a person could become upset with his spouse because she left the bedroom a mess, while he may actually be angry at his mother who always said he was sloppy or at his father who always made him clean up after him. Or a person may be angry just because it has been a stressful day in which he has felt out of control.

A person must also learn to control his anger. The saying "Count to ten before you speak" doesn't deny the anger, but it does indicate the necessity of thinking before lashing out.

Using the energy of anger as a resource to get over life's hurdles is a wise choice in all situations in which anger is a factor. Often arising when we are the most tired, anger produces physical and emotional energy. But this energy can be put to constructive use to solve problems and to do what may seem impossible.

One last word on anger. People wonder if it is all right to be angry with God. When we read Psalm 88, we hear Bible writers express anger without sin or lack of faith. In fact, becoming angry with God is a healthy sign of closeness and dependence on him. It acknowledges that we cannot save ourselves and that God is in control.

Anger is relational. We only get angry with other persons. The closer our relationship, the more intense our anger. Love for God demands honesty. If we can't be honest with God, what kind of relationship do we have with him? Our anger toward God is not rejection but a cry for understanding. It comes from our limitations, frustrations, and hurts.

Restoration and healing are always the biblical objectives of expressing anger. When hurts go deep, believing that God is still there and still cares for us requires much faith. Revealing our inner experiences and feelings to God indicates trust; hiding them only shows lack of trust.

Someone may say that it is all right to get angry with God because he will forgive. But there is nothing to forgive because anger is not a sin. God is a person we love and who loves us. We should have such a close relationship that we can go to God in our anger, knowing that he will help us to resolve it and that he will heal our hurt.

THE HISTORY OF BATTERED WOMEN IN THE CHURCH

Writing in 1869, John Stuart Mill called on people to consider the tragedy being played out every day in their homes, a tragedy that still goes on today.

The sufferings, immoralities, evils of all sort, produced in innu-merable cases by the subjection of individual women to individ-ual men, are far too terrible to be overlooked. . . . And it is per-fectly obvious that the abuse of power cannot be very much checked while the power remains. It is a power given or offered, not to good men, or decently respectable men, but to all men, the most brutal and the most criminal. . . . The law of servitude in marriage is a monstrous contradiction to all the principles of the modern world. . . . It is the sole case, now that slavery has been abolished, in which a human being in the plenitude of every faculty is delivered up to the tender mercies of another human being, in the hope forsooth that this other will use the power solely for the good of the person subjected to it. . . . Marriage is the only actual bondage known to our law. There remain no legal slaves except the mistress of every house.

Too many statistics can be overburdening, but domestic violence is so foreign to and so often ignored in the church that we need to face what is going on around us as well as among us. Domestic violence is not just something reported in the newspaper but a hidden secret in many Christian homes.

People are more likely to be physically assaulted, beaten, and killed in their own home by a loved one than any place else or by anyone else in society. The FBI reports that a spousal beating occurs every twelve seconds in the United States. In ninety-five percent of the homes the beatings are inflicted by men, and in the remaining five percent both the husband

and wife are violent. It is estimated that between three and four million wives are battered each year, and twenty-five percent of all wives can expect to be beaten some time in their married lives. There are more injuries requiring medical attention due to spousal abuse than to rape, auto accidents, and muggings combined. Abused women make up twenty percent of all women treated in hospital emergency rooms.

Spousal abuse goes far beyond bruises and broken bones. The FBI reports that thirty percent of all female homicide victims were killed by a husband or boyfriend. A study done in Detroit and Kansas City revealed that in eighty-five to ninety percent of partner homicides, the police intervened at least once in the two years prior to the murder, and in more than half the cases they were called to intervene at least five times. The Cook County Women's Correctional Facility reports that forty percent of the women who were convicted of murder or manslaughter were abused. All of these women had sought help from the police at least five times before resorting to homicide.

These statistics reveal a crisis that exists in many homes and across all racial and economic groups. In fact, contrary to popular perception, there is a much higher percentage of spousal abuse in white families than in all ethnic minorities, and wife beating is viewed as more acceptable as educational levels rise.

An unfortunate fact of life for centuries, wife beating is not a recent phenomenon. It is also not the result of the breakdown of the traditional family, the rebellion of the 60s, the "me" generation of the 70s, or the yuppyism of the 80s. The mentality that produced this brutality is not only found in secular society but in the Christian church as well.

Some of the roots of today's domestic violence can be traced back to the early church fathers. Theologians who shaped western Christianity were greatly influenced by the dualistic separation of spirit and matter in Plato's philosophy, which taught that what is associated with the spirit is good and what is associated with matter is evil. Plato said that the spiritual quest of humankind is to rise above the bonds of matter and to seek truth through "pure and unadulterated thought." He taught that we must cut ourselves off from the senses, which Plato called an "impediment preventing the soul from attaining truth and clear thinking."

Theologically, this repudiation of matter produced a pessimistic view of the body. It also fostered an antisexuality that included a bias against women and ultimately provided the ecclesiastical sanction for violence against them.

The mixing of Platonic philosophy and biblical dictums presented the early church fathers with a problem—the Bible does not teach a mind-body dualism. Although the Jews had a male-dominated culture, the Old Testament clearly teaches that the creation is good; it affirms the body and sexuality and tells us that marriage is a gift from God. The apostle Paul also teaches the goodness of creation and the wholeness of the person in the unity of body, mind, and spirit. The church fathers could not biblically teach two creations—one spiritual and good, the other material and evil.

Women, therefore, became the scapegoats. Because the soul's flight from the body was a precondition for salvation, these theologians concluded that the body must be the source of human sin. And because it was the woman who sinned first and presented the man with a "body" problem, they concluded that sexuality, specifically female sexuality, was the cause of the soul's descent into perdition. Augustine reflected this devaluation of women when he wrote:

> A good Christian is found in one and the same woman to love the creature of God whom he desires to be transformed and renewed, but to hate in her the corruptible and mortal conjugal connection, sexual intercourse and all that pertains to her as a wife.

For many Christian thinkers marriage was viewed as a necessity, but celibacy was viewed as a higher and holier calling. Jerome wrote, "I praise marriage and wedlock, but only because they beget celibates; I gather roses from thorns, gold from the earth, pearls from shells."

Historically, theological discussions about the dignity of persons have centered in the concept of the image of God. We have dignity and worth and are called the crown of God's creation because we were created male and female in God's image. For the early church fathers, however, the woman did not have the capacity to bear the image of God by herself. Again quoting Augustine:

> When I was treating of the nature of the human mind, I have said already that the woman together with her husband is in the image of God so that the whole substance may be one image. But when she is referred to separately in her quality as a helpmate which regards woman alone, then she is not the image of God. But as regards the man alone, he is the image of God as fully and completely as when woman too is joined with him in one.

The devaluation of women continued into the Middle Ages. The "power of correction" or "right of chastisement," as it was called, gave religious and legal sanction for the absolute control of man, who represented the mind, over the woman, who represented the body. That control even included physical violence. This discipline was viewed as beneficial to the woman and the only hope she had of retaining her salvation.

The Council of Toledo in A.D. 400 declared that "a husband is bound to chastise his wife moderately, unless he is a cleric, in which case he may chastise her harder." A later passage states that "if wives of clergy transgress their commands, they may beat them, keep them bound in their house and force them to fast but not unto death."

The "Rules for Marriage" compiled by Friar Cherubino and instituted for the city of Sienna between 1450 and 1481 stated:

When you see your wife commit an offense, don't rush at her with insults and violent blows; rather first correct the wrong lovingly. . . . but if your wife is of a servile disposition and has a crude shifty spirit, so that pleasant words have no effect, scold her sharply, bully and terrify her. And if this still doesn't work . . . take up a stick and beat her soundly. . . for it is better to punish the body and correct the soul than to damage the soul and spare the body.

Although the reformers Luther and Calvin expressed greater appreciation for the female sex, they did not depart from the view historically held by the church. Maintaining a negative posture toward sexuality and seeing women as a shameful necessity for the outlet of uncontrollable human impulses, Luther stated, "We cannot hardly speak of her without a feeling of shame." Sexuality, for Luther, was a consequence of human disgrace and sin, and woman was the primary focus of this human weakness. Although the male impulses were what presumably troubled him, he projected this weakness onto women, saying that they were not in control of themselves:

Women are ashamed to admit this, but scripture and life reveal that only one woman in thousands has been endowed with a god-given aptitude to live in chastity and virginity. A woman is not fully the master of herself.

Luther also perpetuated the view that women were not equal to men in the reflection of God's image. Speaking of Eve, Luther insisted that "although she was a most extraordinary creature similar to Adam, as far as the image of God is concerned, she was nevertheless a woman . . . [and although] she was a most beautiful work of God, she nevertheless was not equal to the male in glory and prestige."

Since the woman, according to Luther, was deficient in her capacity to image God, she was assigned a subordinate role in life:

The woman bears subordination just as unwillingly as she bears those pains and inconveniences that have been placed upon her flesh. The rule remains with the husband and the wife is compelled to obey him by God's command. He rules the home and the state, wages war, defends his possessions, tills the soil, builds, plants, etc. The woman on the other hand, is like a nail driven into the wall. She sits at home and for this reason Paul in Titus 2 called her a domestic.

Although he never addressed the problem of battered women directly, Luther clearly believed wifely insubordination required physical discipline. Speaking of his own wife he said, "Whenever Katie gets saucy, she gets nothing but a box in the ear."

John Calvin gave special emphasis to compatibility in marriage, but the arrangement was clearly hierarchical not egalitarian. Marital stability depended on the wife's subordination to her husband, and any rebellion was considered disruptive of the God-given pattern for family relationships. Calvin was sympathetic to the plight of battered women, but his reply to a woman seeking help in an abusive situation reflects his traditional position:

> We have special sympathy for women who are evilly and roughly treated by their husband, because of the roughness and cruelty of the tyranny and captivity which is their lot. We do not find ourselves permitted by the Word of God, however, to advise a woman to leave her husband, except by force of necessity; and we do not understand this force to be operative when a husband behaves roughly and uses threats to his wife, not even when he beats her, but only when there is imminent peril to her life, whether from the persecution by the husband or by his conspiring. . . . We exhort her to bear with patience the cross which God has seen fit to place upon her; and meanwhile not to deviate from the duty which she has before God to please her husband, but to be faithful whatever happens.

When the first northern European settlers came to this country, the situation had not changed. European Common Law held to the "rule of thumb" principle that a man had the right to "whip his wife provided that he use a switch no thicker than his thumb." The popular Napoleonic Code notion—"a woman, a spaniel, and a walnut tree, the more you beat 'em, the better they be"— reinforced the social approval of violence against women.

When the early church fathers departed from the Bible and adopted the mind-body dualism, they introduced within the Christian tradition a further devaluation and abuse of women. The cries against this evil, both inside and outside Christianity, went virtually unheard.

A sad by-product of the mind-body dualism is that men are deprived of many of the good things associated with the body, such as the capacity for emotion and sensuality. Men are asked to live with an inner alienation that both misshapes their individual and collective self-concept and limits their ability to live in a true loving relationship with others.

Appendix C

THE ROD OF DISCIPLINE

Physical abuse has been around for centuries in both the Christian and non-Christian communities. A phrase often bantered about by those who advocate the rough treatment of children is "spare the rod and spoil the child." That is not a direct quotation from the Bible but is based on Proverbs 13:24: "He who spares the rod hates his son, but he who loves him is careful to discipline him" (NIV). Many assumed that the rod mentioned here is a stick, paddle, belt, or whatever is used to beat and discipline another person.

The rod of Proverbs 13:24 is, however, the same rod mentioned in Psalm 23, "Your rod and staff, they comfort me." The Hebrew word "shabat" is used in both passages. A "shabat," used by a shepherd in caring for the sheep, had five practical uses.

1. It was a symbol of the shepherd's guardianship over the sheep.
2. It could be thrown with great accuracy just beyond wandering sheep to send them scurrying back to the flock.
3. It could be used to ward off an intruder and protect the sheep from any attacking animal.
4. It was used to count the sheep as they "passed under the rod."
5. It was used to part the wool in order to examine the sheep for disease, wounds, or defects which needed treatment.

There is no evidence that the rod was ever used to strike the sheep. The rod therefore stands as a symbol for all correction, for firm yet loving discipline. We could interpolate from the uses of the shepherd's "shabat" five parental guidelines for discipline.

1. Discipline should bring security into the lives of our children. They should know that they are cared for, loved, and accepted.
2. Discipline should be a means of guidance. A loving parent will teach the child to keep him or her from going astray.
3. Discipline should have an element of protection from outsiders who would seek to harm the child.
4. Discipline should provide a way of evaluating the progress of each child toward self-sacrificing love.
5. Discipline should include a way of diagnosing anxieties within the child and provide ways for healing.

Thus the rod of discipline should be a source of comfort, not a form of fear and intimidation. Paul understands the Old Testament idea of discipline when he reminds fathers in Ephesians 6:4, "Fathers, do not exasperate your children; instead, bring them up in the training and instruction of the Lord." In Colossians 3:21 he says, "Fathers, do not embitter your children, or they will become discouraged."

Discouragement is "the plague of the youth." Therefore, all discipline must have an element of encouragement in it. Physical abuse can never encourage.

BIBLIOGRAPHY

Anderson, Ray S. "The Pastoral Role in Crisis Counseling." Fuller Theological Seminary, 1990.

_____. "Christian Perspectives on Death and Dying." Fuller Theological Seminary, 1990.

_____. "Theological Reflection on Domestic Violence." Fuller Theological Seminary, 1990.

Balswick, Jack, and Judith Balswick. *The Family.* Grand Rapids, MI: Baker Book House, 1989.

Beattie, Melody. *Co-Dependent No More.* New York: Harper & Hazeldon, 1987.

Black, Claudia. *It Will Never Happen to Me!* M.A.C., 1982.

Bussert, Joy M.K. *Battered Women: From a Theology of Suffering to an Ethic of Empowerment.* Division for Mission in North America, Lutheran Church in America, 1986.

Carlson, Lee W. *Child Sexual Abuse: A Handbook for Clergy and Church Members.* Valley Forge, PA: Judson Press, 1988.

Clark, Rita-Lou. *Pastoral Care of Battered Women.* Philadelphia: The Westminster Press, 1986.

Fortune, Marie. *Sexual Violence: The Unmentionable Sin.* New York: Pilgrim Press, 1983.

_____. *Keeping the Faith: Questions and Answers for the Abused Woman.* San Francisco: Harper & Row Publishers, 1987.

Herman, Judith Lewis. *Father-Daughter Incest.* Cambridge, MA: Harvard University Press, 1981.

Hille, Sue. "The God of Guidance." *Working Together.* (Fall 1985).

Horton, Anne L., and Judith A. Williamson., eds. *Abuse and Religion: When Praying Isn't Enough.* Lexington, MA: Lexington Books, 1988.

Johnson, Laurene, and Georglyn Rosenfeld. *Divorced Kids: What You Need to Know to Help Kids Survive a Divorce.* Nashville, TN: Thomas Nelson Publishers, 1990.

Tibbits, Richard. "Termination of Treatment Issues." Fuller Theological Seminary, 1990.

_____. "The Dying Patient." Fuller Theological Seminary, 1990.

_____. "Death: Part of Living." Fuller Theological Seminary, 1990.

_____. "Grief." Fuller Theological Seminary, 1990.

_____. "Anger: A Resource for the Energy Crisis." Fuller Theological Seminary, 1990.

_____. "Grief-Complicated." Fuller Theological Seminary, 1990.

Swihart, Judson J., and Gerald C. Richardson. *Counseling in Times of Crisis.* Waco, TX: Word Books, 1987.

Switzer, David K. *The Minister as Crisis Counselor.* (Rev. Ed.) Nashville, TN: Abingdon Press, 1986.

Wegscheider, Sharon. *Another Change: Hope and Health for the Alcoholic Family.* Palo Alto, CA: Science and Behavior, 1981.

Wolfert, Alan D. *Death and Grief: A Guide for Clergy.* Muncie, IN: Accelerated Development Inc. Publishers, 1988.

Wright, H. Norman. *Crisis Counseling: Helping People in Crisis and Stress.* San Bernardino, CA: Here's Life Publishers Inc., 1985.

_____. *How to Have a Creative Crisis.* Waco, TX: Word Books, 1986.

_____. *Beating the Blues: Overcoming Depression and Stress.* Ventura, CA: Regal Books, 1988.

_____. *Counseling and Testing: Practical Applications.* Santa Ana, CA: Christian Marriage Enrichment, 1988.